MURDER IN THE 33rd DEGREE

Murder
in the
33rd
Degree

by

CHARLES THEODORE MURR

Cover design & illustration
by Enrique J. Aguilar
Illustrations by Enrique J. Aguilar
© 2022 Charles T. Murr
ISBN 9798432706935

SED QUIS CUSTODIET IPSOS CUSTODES?

[But Who Will Guard the Guards Themselves?]

JUVENAL

Roman Poet and Satirist, First Century AD
(Satires; Book VI, Line 347)

DEDICATION

to

His Eminence
ÉDOUARD CARDINAL GAGNON

Faithful Servant of Jesus Christ,
Priest, Bishop,
Loyal Son and Prince of the Church,
Philosopher, Theologian, Lawyer,
Teacher, Linguist,
Mentor, Guide,
Friend.

Contents

FOREWORD TO THE ITALIAN VERSION

By Dr. Roberto de Mattei

I found this book, *Murder in the 33rd Degree*, a fascinating read. Its author, Father Charles Murr, is an American priest who lived, studied, and worked in Rome from 1972 to 1979. These decisive Roman years of his life enabled him to write a wonderful account of many major events that unfolded before his eyes. It is not just the pleasant and engaging narrative style that makes his book so compelling, but the accurate description of the characters and, above all, the disturbing story itself, that of the [1975-1979] investigation into Freemasonry within the Vatican itself, carried out by a highly exemplary prelate. I know some of the facts and knew some of the main characters described in Don Murr's book and can confirm the absolute historical accuracy of the events the author himself witnessed. His is not just a memoir, but a precious historical contribution to better understand the complex reality that is the Roman Curia.

Father Charles Theodore Murr, born in Saint Paul, Minnesota in 1950, was ordained a priest in Rome on May 13th, 1977. It is between 1977 and 1979 that his story unfolds, through fifteen chapters that correspond to memorable meetings and dialogues between the protagonists: Monsignor Mario Marini [1936-2009], Archbishop Giovanni Benelli [1921-1982], Canadian Archbishop Eduoard Gagnon [1918-2007], and the three Popes who succeeded one another in 1978, the year that saw the tumultuous transition from Paul VI's pontificate [1963-1978] to that of

John Paul II [1978-2005], with the brief, one month reign of John Paul I [1978].

Between 1972 and 1974, two prominent cardinals, Dino Staffa and Silvio Oddi, went to Pope Paul VI and formally accused Archbishop Annibale Bugnini (Secretary of the Sacred Congregation for Divine Worship) and Cardinal Sebastiano Baggio (Prefect of the Sacred Congregation for Bishops) of being active Freemasons. At Archbishop Benelli's recommendation, Pope Paul VI entrusted the investigation into the Roman Curia to Archbishop Gagnon, the Rector of the Canadian College, who dedicated himself to the assignment with the seriousness and determination that distinguished him.

On May 16, 1978, a memorable meeting took place between Paul VI, still deeply affected by the assassination of Aldo Moro, and Archbishop Gagnon, who handed him the results of his investigation into the Roman Curia, warning him about the dire seriousness of the situation. The Pope, tired and suffering, asked Gagnon to keep the papers and hand them over to his successor. Pope Paul VI died several months later, on the 6th of August 1978. There were two more meetings, both unsuccessful, between the Apostolic Visitor [Gagnon] and the next two pontiffs.

Father Murr's narrative ends with Archbishop Gagnon's audience with Pope John Paul II in 1979. It was in that same year that I met Doctor Wanda Poltawska, from Krakow, and, through her, in 1980, Monsignor Mario Marini. Poltawska was a very dear friend of the new Pope. She had been miraculously healed from cancer through the prayers of Padre Pio, and it was Father Karol Wojtyla who brought her petition to Padre Pio's attention. It was through Doctor Poltawska that I had the opportunity to meet Pope John Paul II, but above all, to meet the Pope's young personal secretary, Monsignor Stanislaus Dziwisz. Doctor Poltawska told me of the great esteem and admiration Pope John Paul had for Archbishop Gagnon. His esteem was such that, after the assassination attempt on his life, the Pope called Gagnon back to Rome, appointed him President of the Pontifical Council for the Family, and created him a cardinal. When, together with the Marquis Luigi Coda Nunziante, we formed the *Famiglia Domani Association,* we found in him a friend and a supporter. Cardinal Gagnon died on August 25, 2007, and must be regarded as a great defender of the Church, which Father Murr represents well in his book.

In one of the many conversations I had with him, Monsignor Mario Marini told me that when Gagnon went to give John Paul II the results of his Vatican investigation, he made one fatal mistake. Describing the dramatic situation of the Church, Gagnon could not hold back his tears, thus confirming the image that the Secretary of State [Cardinal Jean Villot] had given of him to the Pope: a man in crisis, depressed, deranged, ultimately unreliable. John Paul II listened to Gagnon but would not intervene. After Cardinal Villot's death, Monsignor Marini watched with grave concern as key Vatican positions were given to those thriving in the shadow of John Paul II's new Secretary of State, Cardinal Agostino Casaroli. Marini explained to me, in detail, the existence of what he called a "Mafia", surrounding the Polish Pope. When using the word "Mafia", he always made it clear that the Holy Church remained divine and indefectible, even with Churchmen who serve and betray her.

According to Msgr. Marini, to understand what was happening in the Vatican, one had to go back to the death of Paul VI [August 6, 1978] when two strong regional groups or "clans" were contending for power in the City of the Popes. Marini called them the Lombard-Piedmontese "Family" and the Romagna "Family", attributing to the word "Family" what the Mafia means by *"cosche"*, clans or groups in control of a territory.

Upon the death of Paul VI, the two "Families" entered

a "pact of steel" for control of the Vatican. The director of this agreement was Archbishop Achille Silvestrini, shadow and alter ego of Cardinal Casaroli, whom he had succeeded in 1973 in the secretariat office of Council for Public Affairs of the Church. Silvestrini himself – as Julia Meloni, in an excellent reconstruction of history, presents him to us – is the "mastermind" of the St. Gallen Mafia [The St. Gallen Mafia, Tan, 2021, tr. en., The St. Gallen Mafia, Faith and Culture, 2022]. "Every morning at nine – explained Msgr. Marini – the political group that runs the Vatican, composed of these characters, meets, and prepares its reports for the Pope, but the real decisions have already been made by a hidden "directorate" which effectively controls all information, stored in inaccessible archives, and suitably filtered for the purposes of maneuvering choices and proposing appointments under apparently obvious pretexts." These revelations were published under the pseudonym Romanus, in three articles in the monthly [February, March and April, 1980] issues of *Impact Suisse* magazine. I brought them up in *Corrispondenza Romana*, November 3 and 17, and December 21, 2021.

Msgr. Mario Marini was highly esteemed by subsequent Popes. John Paul II named him a Canon of the Vatican Basilica and Undersecretary of the Sacred Congregation for Divine Worship; Benedict XVI made him Secretary of the Pontifical Commission *Ecclesia Dei*. Like Cardinal Gagnon, Marini was an authentic priest in an era of confusion and apostasy. He did not want to talk further about Gagnon's dossier, sections of which have been lost, leaving many crucial questions regarding Freemasonry within the Vatican.

Regarding my own awareness of this subject, I remember that in early July of 1978 I received a phone call from Princess Eliane Radziwill (1919-2006) who asked to meet me with my friend Agostino Sanfratello to discuss a sensitive matter. Eliane Radziwill was a decreet, but energetic and active woman, for many years, national secretary of the *"Una Voce Italia"* Association, to which she had contributed space in her splendid home on the Via Giulia. To us who had received confidentially a dossier containing the names of some Vatican ecclesiastics and laity allegedly affiliated with Freemasonry, the princess voiced her doubts about the authenticity of the documents. She wanted our opinion on the matter.

We carefully examined the papers she gave us (copies of which I have kept). They contained an alphabetical list of prelates and laity, some of whom held positions in the Vatican. Among them were the names of Cardinal Jean Villot, Secretary of State, Agostino Casaroli, Secretary of the Council for the Public Affairs of the Church, Pio Laghi, Nuncio to Argentina, Annibale Bugnini, Nuncio to Iran, Paul Marcinkus, President of the Works of Religion [a.k.a., the Vatican Bank], Cardinals Ugo Poletti and Leo Suenens, Franco Biffi, Rector of the Lateran University, Don Virgilio Levi, Director of the *Osservatore Romano,* and numerous bishops of various Italian dioceses. In addition to the names, the serial numbers and dates of initiation into Freemasonry were indicated. Bishop Bugnini's initiation date was listed as April 23, 1963, his code number 1365/75, and his code name BUAN.

The documents struck us as extremely amateurish. The letters were all typed, without headings, with clearly apocryphal signatures. An alleged letter to Bugnini, dated July 14, 1964, gave him the task of creating a new religion and spreading de-Christianization "within a decade", with a "fixed salary of 500,000 lire per month which may be increased". No serious conspirators would have expressed themselves in the clumsy manner found in these letters. What to conclude? I had the impression of an operation carried out by Freemasonry itself, or from parties close to it. In my opinion, the papers of which the princess had come into possession, and which were then spread to various circles, were fakes, meant to discredit the serious investigation conducted in the Vatican by Archbishop Edouard Gagnon. On September 12, 1978, the weekly OP *[Osservatore Politico]* directed by journalist Carmine ("Mino") Pecorelli, published an article entitled *La Grande Loggia Vaticana,* a list of 121 names of Vatican officials and high-ranking prelates claiming them as Freemason affiliates. The name of Pecorelli – murdered in Rome on March 20, 1979 – later appeared in the alphabetical list of 962 alleged members of the P2 Lodge of Freemasonry, seized on March 17, 1982, from the "Grand Master" Licio Gelli. The document's source was therefore Masonic, or at least from a branch of Freemasonry.

Masonic infiltrations of the Church are a reality, as real as KGB infiltrations were in the years of the Second Vatican Council. Nonetheless, it is a typical strategy of secret movements to ridicule their adversaries by spreading disinformation or documents that are both true *and* false; documents interwoven in such a way as to muddy the waters. This is why we must treat these matters with caution and balance, without falling into a "conspiracy" mentality which is often a trap set by the secret movements themselves. It is clear from Father Murr's account that such a mentality was completely foreign to Archbishop Gagnon, who approached his delicate mission with tact, integrity, and a commitment to the truth.

The issues raised here are truly grave, but the tone of Father Murr's book is wise and at times even jovial. Although the picture of the Roman Curia that he paints is unsparing, his pages are impregnated with a strong supernatural love for the Church and an authentic "Roman spirit". So, yes, we want our guides to be examples of virtue, we certainly want holy priests and bishops, but the Church, with over two thousand years of experience, can help us accept the tangled coil of virtue and vice that exists in the human heart. Man wants the best, but like his Master, he must be satisfied with what is available. In this, he finds greater wisdom than anything our "cancel culture" has to offer.

ROBERTO de MATTEI

Rome

FOREWORD

By a Friend and Brother Priest

Murder in the Thirty-Third Degree – the title was too good to pass up, but my friend Charles had some qualms about using it because he did not want potential readers to think this is yet another "conspiracy theory" book about the death of Blessed John Paul I. His story does involve Vatican intrigues and Freemasons, and the unexpected death of that pontiff is one of its subplots. But the larger narrative chronicles a noble effort by a dedicated man of the Church to deal with corruption in the Roman Curia. He did this, not as an investigative reporter or "whistle blower," but at the direction of Pope Paul VI himself. Our author was privileged to know this heroic figure, Archbishop Édouard Gagnon, and this friendship gives him a unique vantage point from which to tell his story.

Because Freesmasonry is frequently mentioned in this book, Father Murr has asked me to provide a summary explanation of how the Catholic Church views this secret fraternity. There is a wealth of information (and misinformation, and disinformation!) available to the curious reader. Rather than attempt to describe its complex history (a history made more complex by the solemn secrecy Freemasonry enjoins on its members), I will briefly summarize its broad outlines, and then present the position of the Catholic Church vis-à-vis this organization.

Although Masonic lore traces its history back to the age of the great cathedrals, and even further back to the building of the Temple in Jerusalem, Freemasonry as we know it emerged in the early 18th century and can best be described as a quasi-religious movement espousing Deist principles that promotes an "enlightened" vision of human brotherhood and progress. Many Americans, whose only knowledge of the Masons is that they form fraternal organizations to do good works, are for this reason puzzled about why Catholics are forbidden from joining.

One objection from the Catholic point of view is that Freemasonry has its own unique dogmas, ceremonies, and hierarchy, and many of these conflict with fundamental tenets of Divine Revelation as received and professed by the Catholic Church. More dramatically, Masonic organizations have played an active role in undermining, and indeed persecuting, the Church, especially in traditionally Catholic countries. The *fraternité* of the French Revolution fueled the brutal murders of thousands of innocent Catholic priests, religious, and lay people. Masons have been active in anti-Catholic movements in Europe over the past three hundred years. Closer to home, on our very doorstep in fact, the Masonic government in Mexico waged a bloody war against the Catholic Church (1925-1930). In the city where I live there is a beautiful convent of Carmelite nuns originally from Mexico; the community had to flee their native land to avoid death. These are simply women of prayer, devoted to a life of seclusion, but their very existence was viewed as a threat by the Mexican government. A more recent example of anti-Catholic activity can be found in the 1981 "Vatican Bank Scandal," in which the Italian Freemason Lodge P2 (*"Propaganda Due"*) sought to ruin the central financial administration of the Holy See. I would suggest that this incident lends credence to the concerns raised in this book about the infiltration of Masons into the leadership of the Catholic Church.

Given that at best Freemasonry espouses doctrines inimical to Catholic faith, and that at worst some Masonic groups have actively sought the ruin of the Catholic Church, it is not surprising that the popes have consistently forbidden Catholics to join. The first prohibition was published in 1738 by Pope Clement XII in his encyclical *Eminenti Specula,* and this has been followed by more than twenty similar statements, down to our own time.

This constant prohibition found expression in the 1917 *Code of Canon Law:*

Canon 2335: Those giving their name to masonic sects or other associations of this sort that machinate against the Church or legitimate civil powers contract by that fact excommunication simply reserved to the Apostolic See.

This was the law of the Church when the events recounted in this book took place. Thus, if someone in the Roman Curia was a Freemason, he was by that very fact excommunicated. Archbishop Gagnon's investigation gathered a great deal of evidence about this. One reason Father Murr has written this narrative is to get to the truth: *The only way to settle the question of whether and how many high-ranking Churchmen were Freemasons is for Gagnon's report to be made public.*

The new *Code of Canon Law* promulgated in 1983 made a significant change to Canon 2335:

Can. 1374: A person who joins an association which plots against the Church is to be punished with a just penalty; however, a person who promotes or directs an association of this kind is to be punished with an interdict.

There is no explicit mention of "masonic sects." It would seem that this new canon sought to take into account the experience of Catholics in countries where Freemasonry does not actively seek the destruction of the Catholic Church, and to limit its sanctions to those who join lodges with an anti-Catholic agenda. But even if a particular Masonic organization does not work to bring harm to the Church, there remains the fact that many tenets and practices of Freemasonry are contrary to Catholic faith. For this reason, when the question was raised after the publication of the new Code as to whether

Catholics were still prohibited from joining the Masons, the Congregation for the Doctrine of the Faith issued a brief statement asserting that the prohibition still stands. The rationale for this decision was described at length in an article entitled "Reflections a Year After Declaration of the Congregation for the Doctrine of the Faith: Irreconcilability between Christian faith and Freemasonry," which appeared in *L'Osservatore Romano*, March 11, 1985. I give this commentary in its entirety because it offers the most thorough explanation of the mind of the Church today on the question of Freemasonry:

On 26 November 1983 the S. Congregation for the Doctrine of the Faith (S.C.D.F.) published a declaration on Masonic associations (cf. *AAS* LXXVI [1984], 300). At a distance of little more than a year from its publication, it may be useful to outline briefly the significance of this document.

Since the Church began to declare her mind concerning Freemasonry, her negative judgment has been inspired by many reasons, both practical and doctrinal. She judged Freemasonry not merely responsible for subversive activity in her regard, but from the earliest pontifical documents on the subject and in particular in the Encyclical *Humanum Genus* by Leo XIII (20 April 1884), the Magisterium of the Church has denounced in Freemasonry philosophical ideas and moral conceptions opposed to Catholic doctrine. For Leo XIII, they essentially led back to a rationalistic naturalism, the inspiration of its plans and activities against the Church. In his Letter to the Italian people *Custodi* (8 December 1892), he wrote: "Let us remember that Christianity and Freemasonry are essentially irreconcilable, so that enrolment in one means separation from the other."

One could not therefore omit to take into consideration the positions of Freemasonry from the doctrinal point of view, when, during the years from 1970 to 1980, the Sacred Congregation was in correspondence with some Episcopal Conferences especially interested in this problem because of the dialogue undertaken by some Catholic personages with representatives of some Masonic lodges which declared that they were not hostile, but were even favorable, to the Church.

Now more thorough study has led the S.C.D.F. to confirm its conviction of the basic irreconcilability between the principles of Freemasonry and those of the Christian faith.

Prescinding therefore from consideration of the practical attitude of the various lodges, whether of hostility towards the Church or not, with its declaration of 26 November 1983 the S.C.D.F. intended to take a position on the most profound and, for that matter, the most essential part of the problem: that is, on the level of the irreconcilability of the principles, which means on the level of the faith, and its moral requirements.

Beginning from this doctrinal point of view, and in continuity, moreover, with the traditional position of the Church as the aforementioned documents of Leo XIII attest, there arise then the necessary practical consequences, which are valid for all those faithful who may possibly be members of Freemasonry.

Nevertheless, with regard to the affirmation of the irreconcilability between the principles of Freemasonry and the Catholic faith, from some parts are now heard the objection that essential to Freemasonry would be precisely the fact that it does not impose any "principles," in the sense of a philosophical or religious position which is binding for all of its members, but rather that it gathers together, beyond the limits of the various religions and world views, men of good will on the basis of humanistic values comprehensible and acceptable to everyone.

Freemasonry would constitute a cohesive element for all those who believe in the Architect of the Universe and who feel committed with regard to those fundamental moral orientations which are defined, for example, in the Decalogue; it would not separate anyone from his religion, but on the contrary, would constitute an incentive to embrace that religion more strongly.

The multiple historical and philosophical problems which are hidden in these affirmations cannot be discussed here. It is certainly not necessary to emphasize that following the Second Vatican Council the Catholic Church too is pressing in the direction of collaboration between all men of good will. Nevertheless, becoming a member of Freemasonry decidedly exceeds this legitimate collaboration and has a much more important and final significance than this.

Above all, it must be remembered that the community of "Freemasons" and its moral obligations are presented as a progressive system of symbols of an extremely binding nature. The rigid rule of secrecy which prevails there further strengthens the weight of the interaction of signs and ideas. For the members this climate of secrecy entails above all the risk of becoming an instrument of strategies unknown to them.

Even if it is stated that relativism is not assumed as dogma, nevertheless there is really proposed a relativistic symbolic concept and therefore the relativizing value of such a moral-ritual community, far from being eliminated, proves on the contrary to be decisive.

In this context the various religious communities to which the individual members of the lodges belong can be considered only as simple institutionalizations of a broader and elusive truth. The value of these institutionalizations therefore appears to be inevitably relative with respect to this broader truth, which instead is shown in the community of good will, that is, in the Masonic fraternity.

In any case, for a Catholic Christian, it is not possible to live his relation with God in a twofold mode, that is, dividing it into a supraconfessional humanitarian form and an interior Christian form. He cannot cultivate relations of two types with God, nor express his relation with the Creator through symbolic forms of two types. That would be something completely different from that collaboration, which to him is obvious, with all those who are committed to doing good, even if beginning from different principles. On the one hand, a Catholic Christian cannot at the same time share in the full communion of Christian brotherhood and, on the other, look upon his Christian brother, from the Masonic perspective, as an "outsider."

Even when, as stated earlier, there were no explicit obligation to profess relativism as doctrine, nevertheless the relativizing force of such a brotherhood, by its very intrinsic logic, has the capacity to transform the structure of the act of faith in such a radical way as to become unacceptable to a Christian, "to whom his faith is dear" (Leo XIII).

Moreover, this distortion of the fundamental structure of the act of faith is carried out for the most part in a gentle way and without being noticed: firm adherence to the truth of God, revealed in the Church, becomes simple membership, in an institution, considered as a particular expressive form alongside other expressive forms, more or less just as possible and valid, of man's turning toward the eternal.

The temptation to go in this direction is much stronger today, inasmuch as it corresponds fully to certain convictions prevalent in contemporary mentality. The opinion that truth cannot be known is a typical characteristic of our era and, at the same time, an essential element in its general crisis.

Precisely by considering all these elements, the Declaration of the Sacred Congregation affirms that membership in Masonic associations "remains forbidden by the Church," and the faithful who enrolls in them "are in a state of grave sin and may not receive Holy Communion."

With this last statement, the Sacred Congregation points out to the faithful that this membership objectively constitutes a grave sin and by specifying that the members of a Masonic association may not receive Holy Communion, it intends to enlighten the conscience of the faithful about a grave consequence which must derive from their belonging to a Masonic lodge.

Finally, the Sacred Congregation declares that "it is not within the competence of local ecclesiastical authorities to give a judgment on the nature of Masonic associations which would imply a derogation from what has been decided above." In this regard, the text also refers to the Declaration of 17 February 1981, which already reserved to the Apostolic See all pronouncements on the nature of these associations which may have implied derogations from the Canon Law then in force (Can. 2335). In the same way, the new document issued by the S.C.D.F. in November 1983 expresses identical intentions of reserve concerning pronouncements which would differ from the judgment expressed here on the irreconcilability of Masonic principles with the Catholic faith, on the gravity of the act of joining a lodge and on the consequences which arise from it for receiving Holy Communion. This disposition points out that, despite the diversity which may exist among Masonic obediences, in particular in their declared attitude towards the Church, the Apostolic See discerns some common principles in them which require the same evaluation by all ecclesiastical authorities.

In making this Declaration, the S.C.D.F. has not intended to disown the efforts made by those who, with the due authorization of this Congregation, have sought to establish a dialogue with representatives of Freemasonry. But since there was the possibility of spreading among the faithful the erroneous opinion that membership in a Masonic lodge was lawful, it felt that it was its duty to make known to them the authentic thought of the Church in this regard and to warn them about a membership incompatible with the Catholic faith.

Only Jesus Christ is, in fact, the Teacher of Truth, and only in him can Christians find the light and the strength to live according to God's plan, working for the true good of their brethren.

The foregoing article expresses clearly the contemporary threat of Freemasonry: not so much as an anti-clericalist cabal seeking to wrest political power from the Church (although the activities of "P 2" show that this spirit is still active in some quarters), but rather Freemasonry as a humanist movement which, while evoking "The Divine Architect," in fact pursues secular, self-described "Enlightenment" goals. The political role of the Church has changed over the past one hundred and fifty years. Her enemies today are for the most part those who would build a human community without God, and certainly without Christ and His Body, the Church.

The sudden death of Pope John Paul I prompted a variety of conspiracy theories. Combine "Vatican intrigue" with "Masonic plots," and it is not surprising that some suggested that he was murdered to prevent him from moving against Masons working in the Roman Curia. The revelations of the intrigues against the Vatican Bank a few years later suggest that the accusation is not as outrageous as it might first sound. But, as Father Murr tells us, even the man who was most familiar with the extent of Masonic infiltration into the Curia, Archbishop Édouard Gagnon, did not believe that the recently-elected pontiff was murdered. Whether his fatal heart attack had any connection with his meeting with Cardinal Baggio on the night of his death must remain a matter of speculation.

What is decidedly *not* simply a matter of speculation is the contention that some members of the Roman Curia were (are?) Masons. Or better, *it will remain a matter of speculation until Archbishop Gagnon's findings are made public.* When opening the Vatican Archives to scholars, Pope Leo XIII famously stated that "The Catholic Church has nothing to fear from the truth of history." The "Gagnon Papers" were the result of much hard work, often carried out in the face of great opposition. They were produced by a man who loved both the Church and truth. Those who also love both can rightly ask that his findings must be made known. To continue concealing them will only feed the speculations of conspiracy theorists and increase an atmosphere of distrust.

The question might be asked: apart from shedding

some light on a corner of recent history, is the revelation that high-ranking Churchmen were/are connected with Freemasonry important? We will not have the answer to that question, of course, until the extent of Masonic infiltration is made known. I would suggest one significant ramification in connection with the liturgy of the Roman Rite. Critics of the post-conciliar reforms argue that in many cases the "reform" called for by the Fathers of the Second Vatican Council in fact led to a "replacement" which wiped away time-honored liturgical traditions handed on faithfully for many centuries. One can lament or applaud the changes to Catholic worship since the Council; no one can deny that they represent the jettisoning of liturgical traditions on a scale unique in the history of the Church. In the words of Joseph Gelineau, S. J., who served on the Consilium to reform the liturgy, "To tell the truth, it is a different liturgy of the Mass. This needs to be said without ambiguity. The Roman rite as we knew it no longer exists." [*Demain la Liturgie* (Paris: Les Editions du Cerf), p. 77-8] *If* the man at the helm of the project, Archbishop Annibale Bugnini, was in fact a Mason, this could help explain why his Consilium produced texts so at variance with centuries of liturgical practice. Did the architect of "the new Mass" seek to give the Church an ecumenical, enlightened liturgy that appealed to "modern sensibilities" at the expense of fidelity to the *Lex orandi* of the Roman Rite? Such a goal can be explained in part by the *zeitgeist* of the '60's ... but it also expresses the ideals advocated by Freemasonry: a humanity that strives to leave behind the limitations of outworn creed and dogma to forge a new, "supraconfessional" humanity. Whether or not Archbishop Bugnini was in fact a Mason matters very much: if he was, then the liturgical reforms carried out after the Council may have been infected with Masonic doctrines, doctrines inimical to the Revelation entrusted by God to his Church. This in turn can help us better understand, if not the fissure through which the "smoke

XXX

of Satan has entered into the temple of God," at least the chasm dividing those who see the Second Vatican Council as an expression of ongoing Catholic Tradition from those who celebrate it as the beginning of a new Church. The Council called for the Church to enter into sincere dialog with the modern world – but this dialog should not require a secret handshake.

PREFACE

There is a special magic about the first year after a man is ordained a priest; I am sure this is also the experience of newlyweds. You have followed your heart and made a commitment for life. The dreams and "what ifs" are now realized! The experiences of that first year remain green throughout the unfolding years.

It was an added joy for me that I spent that year in Rome, the Eternal City that holds a unique place in the hearts of Catholics. Like most others, I will never forget the first time I beheld the majesty of St. Peter's Basilica, nor the first time I saw with my own eyes the Successor of that humble fisherman chosen by Christ to lead his apostolic band. The Holy Father we call him, and he occupies an important position not only in the structure of the Church, but in the affection of millions of believers. And then there is the city itself, so cherished by saints (and sinners!) down through the ages. What a privilege it was for me, in the first flush of priestly joy, to offer the Holy Sacrifice of the Mass in places sanctified by the relics and memories of the great saints whose roll call is suggested by the names recorded in the Roman Canon.

What I have said so far can be said by any of my brother priests, especially those who had the experience of spending time in the Eternal City with the sacred chrism still fresh on their hands. As such, a memoir such as the one recorded in these pages would be of interest to the family and friends of a priest so singularly blessed. What makes these pages of wider interest, I believe, is the fact that I was there in "the Year of Three Popes", when momentous events were unfolding in Rome. More than that, you will discover as you read that Providence brought me into close association with some remarkable people, whose story has a significance far beyond my own personal connection with them.

For this reason, I would suggest that this is more than just an old priest's recollections of a young priest's adventures. There is much talk these days of needed reforms in the Roman Curia. This was true as well back in 1977-78, and I was granted a unique vantage point: I lived with a man, a truly great man, chosen by the pope himself to carry out such a reform. His name was Édouard Gagnon, a French-Canadian bishop. That his reform efforts were unsuccessful was certainly not his fault: he carried out his mission with integrity, courage, determination, and discretion. He did his utmost to help three successive popes "clean out the stables", but neither he nor they could prevail. Thus, I do not write this simply as a memoir. It is a testimonial to the labors of a man who loved the Church profoundly and took on an unwelcome (indeed, a very distasteful) mission, and his story deserves to be known by all who hold dear the welfare of our holy Mother Church.

Mine is an unabashedly partisan narrative. I am not a historian seeking to present a coolly objective account of the currents – religious, cultural, and social – of that momentous year. My friends were involved in the mess, and they got hurt. I take their side without apology. In these pages you will read about antipathy, jealousy, turf wars, power plays. Are these why reform is desperately needed? Well, yes and no. Of course, such attitudes and actions are the dark side we all can recognize in ourselves (thank God for frequent confession!), and it is not edifying to find them alive and well in the lives of men dedicated to the service of God and His Church. We expect better from priests, and we should.

At the same time, we should not set our hopes too high. To expect perfection from anyone, even a man of God, betrays ignorance of both human nature and of the Bible. Cardinal Newman once gave a conference entitled, "Men, not Angels, the Priests of the Gospel" (*Discourses to Mixed Congregations*, #3). The apostles themselves, of whom the pope and bishops are the successors, come across at times as petty, befuddled, and jealous. Jesus announces that he is going to Jerusalem to be executed in the most horrible way, and they are talking among themselves about who will get thrones closest to Him when He drives out the Romans. Even on the night of the Last Supper itself, as Our Lord was giving them His very Body and Blood, and washing the feet of these men who were about to betray, deny, and abandon him, there they are arguing about who is most important! So, yes, we want our leaders to be paragons of virtue, we certainly want holy priests and bishops, but the Church has over two thousand years of experience to help us accept the tangled skein of virtue and vice that is the human heart. She wants the best, but, like her Master, has to settle for what's available. In this she shows greater wisdom than our "cancel culture": as a friend observed, we live in a world that permits everything and forgives nothing. This world desperately needs the Gospel, which offers both correction and mercy. It is a sorrow to me that, when dealing with the failings of her leaders, these days the Church seems to ape the anti-evangelical wisdom of the culture around her: talk only to your lawyers and let your spin doctors talk for you.

The human weaknesses, missteps, short-sightedness, pettiness, and so on that are part of my story speak to the *subjective* need for reform in the Roman Curia, as in any human organization. But far more importantly, and the principal reason why I have recorded this memoir, is the need to address the *objective* reform of the central administration of Christ's Church. Archbishop Gagnon was commissioned by Pope Paul VI to investigate the charge that the Curia had been infiltrated by men associated with organizations intent on either the destruction of the

Roman Catholic Church, or at the very least its complete neutralization as a force to oppose secularism and relativism. It had been reported to the Holy Father that very high-ranking, influential prelates were in fact Freemasons. He asked the man I am honored to count among one of my dearest friends and greatest mentors to undertake an investigation. He did so at great personal cost, a price tag I witnessed firsthand.

Archbishop Gagnon compiled an exhaustive dossier which left him in no doubt that these shocking allegations were in fact true. I never saw the contents themselves, of course, and the man was discretion itself: he never discussed his findings with me (or with anyone else, so far as I know). But I did see that the files were hefty: weighty in size, and I presume even weightier in content. Those tomes were presented three times to successive popes, and they now reside somewhere in the archives of the Holy See.

Serious reform of the Curia demands that these documents *must* now be made public. If it is true that the man responsible for nominating bishops all over the world for years was a Mason, that could offer a clue to the crisis of leadership we are experiencing. If it is true that the man entrusted with the momentous liturgical reforms carried out after an Ecumenical Council was guided more by Masonic ideals than by the clear directives of the Council Fathers, this could have infected the Church's worship. Given the association between *Lex orandi* and *Lex credendi*, if the architect of our reformed rites wore a Masonic apron, the liturgical books now in use must receive a serious theological review. And if, as Cardinal Benelli once suggested, these two influential Churchmen were just "the tip of the iceberg", how many other members of the Curia were the subject of Archbishop Gagnon's very thorough and well-documented investigation? We don't know. The answer is to be found in the documents themselves. Only when this information is made known can the needed objective reforms of the Roman Curia be addressed. Holy Father, in the interests of transparency, to further much-needed reform in Rome, and indeed for the very vitality of Christ's Church, I implore you to make public the documents my friend labored so assiduously to provide to your predecessors!

A SEAT AT THE TABLE OF HISTORY

Monday, June 27, 1977

The first bell of the Angelus bonged loud and low from the campanile. A passel of startled pigeons took to flight and disappeared in the azure of a near-perfect Roman sky.

I dropped my cigarette to the cobblestones and stubbed it out while bidding a brief farewell to my friends and coworkers, Silvio and Naldo, and turned to take a shortcut from the Vatican Information Office to the ultramodern papal audience hall, the *Aula Nervi*.

No sooner had I crossed the threshold when I came to an abrupt halt. There before me, in the normally wide-open vestibule, were a series of off-white sheets of canvas. These had been hung from ceiling to floor to create four open-fronted cubicles. And, in the center of each stood a middle-aged man attired in scarlet from the *zucchetto* [skullcap] on his head to the socks on his feet.

Stationed at each of the five lateral panels was a young Swiss Guard attired in Medici red, gold and blue, plumed helmet, spats and boots, and clutching a menacing spear should any miscreant need dissuading. Passing the first booth, I mocked a reverential nod to one of them, my Helvetian friend, *Oberstleutnant* Dominique Tourville, standing stiffly at attention. Bypassing three-quarters of the newly-minted cardinals — Italian, Luigi Ciappi; German, Josef Ratzinger; and African, Bernardin Gantin — I took the last place in the last line of elegantly-attired personages. Everyone in this particular queue was waiting to congratulate the man who for years had served as private secretary, most trusted confidant, and Deputy Secretary of State to His Holiness, Pope Paul VI; the same man named Archbishop of Florence by the same pope, and even more recently — this morning, in fact— elevated by him to the cardinalate: Giovanni Benelli.

Waiting my turn in the Benelli line, I thought back to the first time I met him…

Cortile Belvedere. *Four years ago. Of course, I knew of him long before then. No one in Rome hadn't heard of Giovanni Benelli. Of the half a million Catholic priests in the world, was there one who couldn't name the pontiff's right-hand man?*

True, Cardinal Jean-Marie Villot was the pope's Secretary of State, but it was the Deputy Secretary of State, Giovanni Benelli, who had the greater influence on him. Not surprisingly, Villot's odium for Benelli ran as deep as his sense of his own importance - nor did the Frenchman make an effort to conceal either. Villot's envy of the younger and more brilliant Benelli accounted for much of the antipathy between them, but the undisputable dissimilarities between them had far more to do with diametrically opposed ideologies than with conflicting temperaments. More on this a little later.

A dignitary and his wife — the woman in front of me referred to them as "the Peruvian and 'Mrs. Ambassador'" — retreated after taking a photo with Benelli, and I advanced two paces. My memory shifted from that first brief encounter to a far more significant meeting that had taken place just over a month ago. Even as it was happening, I knew that I would never forget that dinner.

It had all started with a phone call at eleven o'clock from my friend Monsignor Mario Marini. He was calling from the office.

"That's right," he said, "An afternoon in the country. Let's get out of the city for a few hours," the deep bass voice half ordered, half coaxed, "We leave at four-thirty. You've never been to Lago di Bracciano?" he asked rhetorically, "The peace. The fresh air. And, oh-o-o-o-oh, Charlie!" he chuckled

Giovanni Cardinal Benelli

with anticipatory delight, "The best tagliatelle ai porcini *and grilled whitefish this far south of* La Romagna!*"*

"Just a minute," I managed to get in a word, "What is it we're celebrating?"

"Humph!" he retorted, "Since when do two good friends need a transcendental reason to get together, to escape the maddening noise of the city, and to enjoy a simple dinner in each other's company?"

"I don't suppose they do. It's just that …"

"Good." he spoke over me, "Holy Office entrance, 4:45," he said and, as was his custom, immediately hung up.

Telephone protocol was not Mario's forte. He didn't like phones. Never trusted them.

Something was up. That much I was sure of. In all our Roman years of friendship Mario Marini had never remained working in the Secretariat of State after hours, that is, without eating lunch and — far more important to him than pranzo — without taking a siesta! Don't get me wrong; in all of Vatican City, you couldn't find a more dedicated and diligent worker than Don Mario Marini. Daily, when he returned home from the Secretariat of State, he brought with him a stack of homework and proceeded to dedicate five or six extra hours to addressing delicate matters of State for the Holy See. But that my noble mentor was willing to forego his forty-minute daily siesta was next to impossible for me to believe. It was — it was against his religion!

No, something was definitely up.

Again, the line shortened and I inched a little closer to the newly-created Cardinal Benelli.

When Mario and I arrived at Lago di Bracciano we took advantage of the extended daylight and went sightseeing around the lake. He pointed out the old summer residences of the American and German Colleges on the hill. Long ago I stopped using words like "quaint" and "charming" to describe Italian hamlets, villages, towns, countryside scenes - even ancient and medieval sectors of large Italian cities. That said, the little town of Bracciano, the tranquil waters of the lake, the setting sun and the very atmosphere were dreams made real.

We got off the main road and onto a much narrower and winding one that brought us into the village of Anguillara and the Chalet del Lago. Mario parked his yellow Fiat and insisted we take a walk along the shore.

Eventually we made our way back to the rustic Chalet. I

noticed a second car, a navy-blue sedan, now parked near ours. I followed Mario into what seemed an empty restaurant made almost completely of wood. With the red sun setting on the lake, wooden walls and knotty pine beams, we could have been in the north of my native Minnesota. Looking around, I smiled to see several tables and chairs covered with cheesecloth and, draped over the chair-backs, large round sheets of pasta set out to dry.

"I told you, the tagliatelle are fresh and homemade," Mario proudly announced.

Just then an older gentleman appeared from the kitchen and, wiping his hands with a white towel, walked over to us. "Buona sera, Monsignore," he greeted Marini, raising his still wet hands, a sort of silent apology for not shaking his. Obviously, this was the owner and, just as obviously, he and Mario knew each other. "You are expected, Monsignore," the owner told Mario and pointed to his right, "The corner table."

Mario turned toward the windows facing the placid lake and took a few steps in that direction, and then a broad smile came to his face. There, in the red glow of the setting sun sat the Vatican Deputy Secretary of State, Bishop Giovanni Benelli, and the former Head of Personnel for the Secretariat, now Deputy-Secretary in the Congregation for the Clergy, Monsignor Guglielmo Zannoni. A moment later, the Vatican minutante [curial official], Don Mario Marini, and his astounded young American sidekick, me, were seated at table with them.

Straightaway, a caveat came to me out of the blue: "Better to remain silent and be thought a fool than to speak and remove all doubt," and, at once, I made a conscious effort to follow this prudent advice.

Given that the three men before me had known each other for years and worked together, the exchange of general pleasantries was brief. Then the question-and-answer session. Where was I born? Were my parents still alive? What did my father do for a living? What was I studying? When was I ordained?

It was Monsignor Zannoni who mentioned that Cardinal Felici had recently ordained me. "A brilliant lawyer and superb classicist, His Eminence," Benelli complimented Felici. "And Archbishop Édouard Gagnon preached at the ordination, in Italian, English and French," Zannoni added. Almost imperceptibly, but not quite, Giovanni Benelli did not follow up on that last bit of information but steered the conversation in another direction. There was something about Gagnon that seemed to bother him. Perhaps they were at odds?

But right before the evening ended, as he was bidding a goodnight to Mario, Benelli's true respect and esteem for the French-Canadian archbishop made itself known. "Tell our friend, Gagnon, that not a day goes by that he is not in my prayers. Tell him, I pray God keeps him strong and safe from all harm. Make sure you tell him that from me, please."

On the ride home, I asked Mario to explain the awkward conversational moment at table, and what Archbishop Benelli's cryptic message for Archbishop Gagnon meant. Mario began by explaining why Archbishop Édouard Gagnon – with whom he and I usually formed a lively trio – was not invited to this particular meal.

"He hasn't finished the Papal Visitation [i.e., Investigation of the Roman Curia]," Mario explained. "For the sake of honesty, and for the sake of appearing honest, Benelli can't speak with Gagnon until he's completed the investigation and handed over his final report to the pope. And, as you know, Gagnon's not finished... Not yet... In case you're still wondering about it," Marini said with a satisfied grin, "Benelli thinks the world of Gagnon; of his intelligence, his honesty, and his integrity. He wouldn't have given this extraordinary assignment to anyone else... Enough said," he said.

So, it was Giovanni Benelli who proposed Édouard Gagnon for Papal Visitor to the Roman Curia; Benelli who convinced Pope Paul VI that Gagnon was the best man for the job; Benelli who, for honesty's sake, could no longer communicate with Gagnon until he finished the critical and delicate task assigned him. Now I understood. Not only did I finally understand, but the great admiration I already had for both men rose higher still.

"Home," by the way, was the Lebanese Residence on Monteverde Vecchio, just off the Gianicolo Hill. There, Archbishop Édouard Gagnon, Monsignor Mario Marini and I lived together in liberty, fraternity, and exceedingly good humor (rather than illusionary equality.)

Finally, I was at the head of the reception line - and with no one behind me, at its tail-end as well.

The man in red and I made eye contact. A full smile came to the round Tuscan face as he gestured *"Avanti"* with his right hand. I approached and made an awkward half-genuflection. "Charles Murr, *Sua Eminenza;"* I reintroduced myself and continued in Italian, "I'd hoped to be among the very first to congratulate you today, but I seem to be the very last."

"Don Char-lie," Benelli exaggerated my very American-ringing first name, *"Fratellino dal nostro Don Marini [Little brother of our Father Marini],"* he said with two or three affirming head nods. "Anguillara," he added, as emphatically as an "Amen" to a prayer.

"What a memory you have, Eminence!"

"A very handy thing, a good memory," he affirmed, "People, places, things, events great and small — they should all of them be remembered," he said, "And above all *people!*" he emphasized. "Take, for example, the date of your ordination," he said with a grin. Then, glancing upward, he tapped his index finger on his right temple: "Friday," he began, "Friday, the thirteenth of May, in this Year of Our Lord, nineteen-hundred and seventy-seven. Am I close?!"

"Wow!" I exclaimed with that very Yankee expression of astonishment, "Memory's one thing," I exclaimed, "But how did you even *know* that to remember it?!"

I never doubted Benelli's reputation as an organizational genius, but the reason for his nickname, *"Sua Efficienza" [His Efficiency]"* was becoming crystal clear.

"At table," he answered straight away, "Monsignor Zannoni remarked how beautiful your ordination was. I asked when you were ordained, and you answered: 'Friday, the thirteenth of May.' The connection between your ordination and my own baptism was effortless. A different year, of course," he grinned and raised his eyebrows slightly, "I wasn't twenty-four hours-old when I was baptized. Now, *you* ask *me* when that was."

"And when was that, *Eminenza?*" I obliged.

"The year: 1921. The day: May the thirteenth. And, as coincidence would have it, Don Charlie," he put his right hand on my shoulder, "in 1921, the thirteenth of May fell on a Friday. So, you see: for me to forget such a thing as your ordination date would actually be harder than trying to remember it."

"Impressive, all the same," I said with admiration, "impressive and humbling."

"Humbling? That your memory is not as good as mine?" he questioned.

"No, Your Eminence; that Cardinal Giovanni Benelli would remember my name *and anything* about me. Humbling," I repeated.

State-of-the-art lighting and neutral canvas backdrops made the red of Benelli's cassock appear more striking still. Or, was it Giovanni Benelli himself? Power, faith and genius transfigured. Then, as during the dinner at *Lago di Bracciano*, I knew I was in the presence of greatness; face to face, one on one, with Giovanni Cardinal Benelli; Archbishop of Florence and, very possibly, Christ's next Vicar on earth.

Naturally, the new cardinal made a special point of praising his former *minutante:* "More than Don Mario's clear thinking and talents, which are many," he nodded to underscore the sincerity of his words, "it is his faith, well-tested and solid, his insights, and the strength of his convictions. Remarkable," he said admiringly, "You have a great teacher and friend in Don Mario," he said in all earnestness and, if I was not mistaken, with a faint trace of honest envy — if, indeed, such a virtuous vice exists. "No doubt about it, *Eminenza*," I answered, "I've been blessed *and* spoiled."

"You both must come to visit me in Florence," he offered. I promised we would. Then he asked in perfect English: "Could I ask a favor of you, Don Charlie? Would you be so kind," he asked, and pointed to a side-table with commemorative cards and booklets, "as to lend a helping hand?" I immediately agreed and the cardinal went toward the corner of the sheeted cubicle for his leather briefcase. Since I was "last man standing," and the cards were in obvious disorder, I understood that I was to gather them up and return them to their boxes. In no time flat, I finished with the cards. I caught Benelli's eye, respectfully raised my hand in a goodbye *salve* and exited the well-staged vestibule.

The dazzling sunshine left me squinting my way from the audience hall to *Piazza Santa Marta* and my parked car. The entire way there, I thought of Benelli's words of praise for that "most worthy teacher" I was blessed with. I thought how radically Mario Marini had changed my life and how much he meant to me. These past four years, not only did I have Mario as my mentor, maestro, counselor, spiritual director and father confessor, above all else, he had become my older brother, my best friend, and the most dramatically positive influence ever in my life. I felt outrageously privileged — because I was!

So, how did this monumental man from Ravenna become my mentor, father, older brother, my friend?

September, 1974. Second floor of the modern, Aztec-inspired, Pontifical Mexican College; near the glass doors to the Guadalupe chapel.

Around eight o'clock that evening, two men, one

larger-than-life, the other slightly "less large," were walking toward me in the corridor. The taller seemed to be in his mid to late thirties, and as he got closer, I saw that he was the same Italian priest who had been introduced to everyone an hour ago, at dinner. He would now be residing at the college.

He stopped in his tracks and, with the enthusiasm of a sailor who has just sighted land, he exclaimed in Spanish: "Oh-o-o-o-o-o-oh! This must be the famous 'Ch-a-llie' I've heard so much about!" His deep bass voice reverberated off the floor-to-ceiling windows. His companion was also in a Roman collar, a Mexican also in his mid-thirties. The Italian, with the broadest smile and exuding bonhomie, walked right up to me, looked me straight in the eyes, and said: "I have it on good authority that a lone *gringo* dwells in these parts," he ribbed good-naturedly, and at once shook my hand, "You must be him!"

"And you must be?" I asked, unsure of his name, though I had heard it an hour before.

"I must be Mario," he answered with a chuckle, "Mario Marini," he said strongly but weakly pronouncing the "r's" in each name, as a Frenchman might pronounce Latin. I noticed it first when he pronounced "Charlie" rather "r-lessly."

"Padre Emilio Berlie-Belaunzaran," the priest next to Don Mario Marini introduced himself, impatiently, as if anxious to get back to the more important matters the two of them had been discussing before stumbling upon me, the proverbial bump in the road.

To be sure, I had never met anyone as straightforward as this Italian cleric, nor anyone with such a commanding presence. His Mexican companion exuded too much of a superior air for me to give him a second thought. But Marini, this Don Mario Marini, I immediately found intriguing — and something told me the feeling was mutual.

Don Mario Marini had returned to Rome after three

Monsignor Mario Marini

years teaching theology in the regional seminary of Chihuahua. He moved into the Mexican College after spending a few days with his family.

After supper the following evening, Don Marini knocked on my door. I was in the middle of an assignment due the next day at the Gregorian University. He insisted I set aside my homework and take a walk and have a coffee with him. With a very warm smile, he forewarned that he would not take no for an answer. He repeated this the next evening, and the evening after that, and every evening thereafter for several weeks. More often than not others joined us, since Marini was the gregarious sort and had an easy way of involving everyone in the conversation.

As for me, I liked it best when it was just him and me. Those nightly walks were much more than just enjoyable; they were thought-provoking and intellectually stimulating. I found myself learning all sorts of things and making sense of many things I knew a little about but by no means enough about; problems stemming from unresolved medieval wars to the stress factors of modern-day bridge building.

I quickly became accustomed to Mario Marini's knock on my door and — though I never said so — really looked forward to hearing it. Those next few months we met regularly, after supper, for the twenty-minute walk to the *Golden Brazil Café* where we'd take a cappuccino and a *Petrus*, and strain to hear one another over "Crocodile Rock" blaring on the backroom jukebox.

"Please, Charlie, I'm tired of asking you to call me 'Mario'," he moaned out comically one evening as we made our customary jaunt. "It's not in me to call a priest by his first name," I answered honestly and respectfully. "Well," he halted his stride in the middle of the crosswalk, "then dig deeper until you find the ability to call a potential friend by his first name. By the way, I like the sound of my name," he said and smiled largely, "I like it almost as much as I like the name 'Charlie.' Almost, but not quite as much," he laughed.

"We're friends, then?" I asked as we resumed our walk.

"Of course not," he snapped, "Not yet, anyway. You studied Aquinas; you know the difference between act and potency."

"Yes. And?"

"Friendship has structure. Rules. Like all good and well-ordered things have. We, you and I, are *potential* friends. If that potential friendship develops, there's a chance we might become *actual* friends," he laughed, but laughed seriously.

Later on, I would discover that Mario —yes, that evening I brought myself to call him by his first name— wrote his second doctoral dissertation on the nature and structure of *Amicitia [Friendship]*.

I was twenty-four. Mario Marini was thirty-seven; thirteen years my senior; younger than my parents by seven years.

Mario and I did not normally converse in Italian or English. Spanish suited our communication needs perfectly. As it was the mother tongue of neither, it put us on equal linguistic footing —equality being a principal tenet of friendship. What's more, it afforded us the freedom to speak openly with each other in public, guaranteeing privacy from eavesdroppers. Truth be told, there was another, slightly devilish plus to speaking Mexican Spanish: we could both cuss —a thing neither of us would do so freely in his own native tongue— with ease and without remorse, since, for all intents and purposes, the swear words meant nothing to us. In fact, they meant very little to the Mexicans themselves, unless spoken in anger.

Little by little, Mario and I learned each other's history, convictions and opinions. It was our logical, pragmatic, and personalist philosophies that united us so deeply. Why wouldn't they? We were both Catholics —fervent Catholics. Our life histories, however, could hardly have been more divergent. My life, I thought, was nothing spectacular. Oldest of seven children. Beautiful parents. Beautiful home. Beautiful home life. Solid Catholic upbringing and formal education. In Rome, now, I thought, to finish a licentiate in philosophy. No immediate plans to marry until finishing law school. Maybe Georgetown?

"And has my American friend ever fallen in love?" Mario once inquired seriously.

"I don't know…" I answered rather offhandedly, "Don't think I ever really *fell* in love… Stepped in it three or four times, but never fell."

By far, Mario Marini's was the more dramatic life — or, should I say, traumatic life? And he didn't seem in any great hurry to tell it. Thinking back on that preliminary, revelatory period of our relationship — now that I'm much older and just a hair wiser — I see that Mario revealed his personal history to me slowly, measuredly, episodically, to let what he was saying sink in, before adding to it. He wanted — I think — to see if I was really "picking up what he was laying down." He was judging my reaction to his revelations every bit of the way. Was I sufficiently empathetic to the obstacles he had faced, dealt with, and overcome in life? Did I appreciate what it cost him to have become a priest?

I did understand, and evidently he saw that I did because, in three months' time, we had learned just about everything there was to learn about each other's life. And I for one never found a single installment of the Mario saga boring. Rich material was there, to be sure, but it was also Mario's way of telling and explaining the twists and turns, the about-faces, the surprises and all the rest, that enticed.

My friend was born on the thirteenth of September, 1936, in Cervia-Ravenna. *Romagnolo* through and through. He had an older sister, Catarina, and a younger brother, Pierpaolo, and though the middle child he was the firstborn male. This, Mario explained — unnecessarily, since I had lived in Italy long enough to witness this phenomenon countless times — was extremely important in Italian family dynamics. More was given to him, and more was expected of him. His father, a civil engineer, dictatorial and cynical by nature, did his best to make life difficult for him — for him and everyone else in the family, but *especially* for him.

His mother, a woman of very strong temperament and even stronger opinions, was tall, tough, seldom smiled and seemed always to have a lit cigarette between her fingers or her lips. I met Mario's joyless progenitors several times and saw firsthand the semi-crippling effect they continued to have on him, even as an adult. In fact, the only times I saw any hint of weakness in my fortress of a friend was when he was in the company of his parents. Individually or jointly — the *mater* and the *pater* were much more effective as a tag-team— they could suck the oxygen out of any joyful occasion, and in no time flat.

The greatest turmoil in the Marini Family was provoked by "religion," or more accurately, was blamed on religion. Mario's parents and both sets of grandparents were dyed–in-the-wool Marxists; his father, a "devout" atheist; his mother, an anticlerical *"mangia-prete"* to the bone. Karl Marx was the sole savior of humanity, and Marxism was the daily *piadina* [flatbread] that nourished the Marini children. Signore and Signora Marini were proud of being very active, card-carrying members of the Italian Communist Party.

At fifteen, Mario's love for soccer got him to join the Catholic Action youth group where, for the first time in his life, he heard the rudiments of Catholicism. Two years later, he asked his parents' permission to go on a weekend camping trip with friends. Instead, he attended a vocation retreat at the Ravenna Seminary. When his father got wind of it, he became furious, marched into the seminary and physically pulled his son out of the retreat. He then grabbed the director by the front of his cassock and threatened to kill him should he or any other priest ever again approach his son.

Upon graduation, his father enrolled him in the School of Engineering at his own *alma mater*, the University of Bologna. He made sure his son was always kept busy —most especially during summer vacations. Through comrades in local government, *L'ingegnere* Marini secured for his son the most coveted job any athletic, good-looking young man could ever hope for: lifeguard on the poshest, most girl-packed beaches on the Adriatic. Meanwhile, Marini senior constantly went out of his way to mock religion, hoping to erase from his son's mind the horrific notion of becoming a priest.

At age 24, Mario Marini finished his doctorate in civil engineering, *magna cum laude*. That same night his mother surprised him with a huge congratulatory party at home. She had taken great pains to invite some of the finest, most beautiful and eligible young ladies of Ravenna. It was time her son Mario went into business with his father, found himself a wife, and started a family.

But that evening her son had a surprise in store for her, too, and for his father, his siblings, and everyone within shouting distance. An hour or so into the party, in the crowded kitchen, Mario Marini made an announcement to all present:

"All my life I've done everything you demanded of me," Mario told his parents, "What I promised to finish, I have finished. Today is the beginning of *my* life." He handed his father the doctoral scroll he had been posing with for photos: "This is what you wanted, *Papa*; it's yours," he said, "with my sincerest thanks for all you've given me. Tomorrow morning, I leave for Milan to start what I wanted to begin six years ago. I've been accepted into the Milan Seminary."

For the very first time in his life, *L'ingegnere* Marini was speechless — speechless but instantly fuming mad. Adding insult to injury, his special guest, the chubby syndicate leader of Ravenna's Communist Party, turned to him and asked incredulously: "A priest? You said he was done with all that." His son's words were like burning coals heaped upon him and the rage inside left him literally unable to speak.

Then, the deafening silence in the kitchen and dining room came to a stingingly abrupt end. *La Signora* Marini, outraged and humiliated before a houseful of guests, hauled off and slapped her son as hard as she could with the back of her broad hand and screamed out a statement that would remain with Mario and all present a lifetime: "Better a slut-whore for a daughter than a filthy priest for a son!"

Early the next morning, "the morning after the night before," following the graduation party to end all graduation parties, without a goodbye to anyone, Mario Marini silently made his way to the Cervia Station and boarded the train for Milan.

"Why Milan? I mean, didn't Ravenna have a seminary?" I had asked him the one and only time he recounted the whole parental horror story. We were seated at the writing desk in his room at the College.

The reasons, he explained, were three.

Knowing the Marini family's strong and multigenerational affiliations to the Communist Party *and* having learned of the threats Mario's father had made on the life of the former seminary rector, the Archbishop of Ravenna decided it would be in everyone's best interests for Mario to study philosophy and theology at a safe distance from Ravenna. Secondly, the young *Dottore* Marini was much older than the average first year philosophy students. In the much larger and better-staffed Seminary of Milan he could receive more personalized academic attention.

"And the third reason?" I asked him.

"Divine Providence," Mario gave the short answer and then proceeded to give the even shorter one: "Money."

Since Signore and Signora Marini had been extremely vocal about severing ties with their son, funding for Mario's seminary education had to be found elsewhere.

When Mario's most unusual circumstances reached the ears of Milan's archbishop, he investigated it further and, finding it true as reported, decided to resolve the difficulty himself. With his own personal funds, the Archbishop of Milan established a theology scholarship for a deserving student. With a second stroke of the pen, he awarded the first scholarship to the young engineer from Ravenna, *Dottore* Mario Marini.

Three years later, Mario's generous benefactor, Archbishop Giovanni Battista Montini, became the sixth pope to take the name of Paul. When Mario completed his studies in Milan, the pope, who had followed his progress from the very beginning, called him to Rome and continued underwriting his studies toward a second doctorate in theology. The pope's trusted friend and his Deputy Secretary of State, Bishop Giovanni Benelli, sent funds from the pontiff's personal account to the Gregorian University, where Mario was enrolled, and to the *Collegio Lombardo*, where he resided. Furthermore, Bishop Benelli saw to it that the "engineer from Ravenna" was granted a personal audience with the pope each Christmas that he might thank him for his ongoing generosity.

In 1966, the day arrived for Deacon Mario Marini to be ordained to the priesthood. The ordination and first Mass took place in his hometown of Cervia-Ravenna. Begrudgingly, his mother was in attendance. Though *Santa Maria Assunta* Cathedral was but a few blocks from the Marini family home, Mario's father, *L'ingegnere* Marini, refused to witness the shame his son was bringing on him and his family.

Like St. Francis before him, Mario Marini had found a true mother in the Church and true fathers in Christ's pastors. How fortunate he was to have Montini and Benelli in his life… How fortunate I was to have Marini in mine…

THE POPE'S BEAST OF BURDEN FINDS A NEW STALL

Sunday, December 4, 1977

"I would 'ave liked to attend," said the French-Canadian. He passed a two-page letter to me and casually explained: "This goes in the Lateran University file, please." He lowered his head slightly and looked at me over his glasses, "...but I 'ave to avoid anything partisan — or anything that could be taken for partisan."

Good-natured, good-looking, strongly willed and strongly built (not an ounce of fat on his 5'10" frame), Archbishop Édouard Gagnon had just moved into the Lebanese Residence with Mario and me. When he and I finished transferring his belongings from the Canadian College to his new room (two doors down from mine), he asked if I could help him, "from time to time," organize the virtual mountain of documentation he had acquired and was continuing to acquire in his investigatory labors. He also asked if, "from time to time," I would drive him to appointments and meetings, especially where time and parking were issues. Gladly, I agreed. The sermon he preached at my ordination was unforgettably beautiful and his great kindness to my mother and father during those special days for them in Rome was above and beyond gracious. All of that aside, Édouard Gagnon's authenticity, his simple charm, honesty and personal sanctity made me want to be in his company as often as he would have me. And when it came to driving him around the city, Archbishop

Gagnon owned the only Fiat in Rome with an automatic transmission, making the hundreds of stop-and-goes shiftlessly easy. What's more, Gagnon's Fiat had Vatican diplomatic plates, which made driving into, around, and "over" Roman traffic a virtual joy! Chauffeuring him was also good for my ego; Gagnon never tired of praising my urban navigational skills: "In the 'eat of Roman traffic, Don Carlo, Mario Andretti's got nothing on you!"

Édouard Gagnon was brilliant yet unassuming, wise beyond his fifty-eight years, a manly gentleman with a delightful sense of humor. As a bishop he was utterly without arrogance, guile or vainglory. A rare and wonderful exception to the Roman rule.

He was one of thirteen children born into a loving family in Montreal. His first major decision in life was choosing between the Catholic priesthood and professional baseball. Obviously, he chose the first, but not to the total exclusion of the latter. After completing his first doctorate, he was named professor of moral theology at *Le Grand Séminaire* of Montreal. As such, each year, June to September, the young professor was free from teaching but not from working. Father Gagnon was sent as summer help to a parish in Brooklyn, New York, which allowed him to frequent Ebbets Field as often as his priestly duties and meager savings permitted. He was and would always remain an avid Dodgers' fan - still (and forever) irritated with Walter O'Malley for moving the club to Los Angeles in 1957, and unwilling to absolve Robert Moses for his part in that catastrophic betrayal.

At 28 Gagnon completed a second doctorate, this one in canon law, from *L'Université de Laval*. After holding various positions in Canada, he was appointed Rector of *El Seminario Mayor de Manizales,* Colombia in 1961 —"the happiest time of my life," he was fond of saying. Three years later he was elected Provincial of the Sulpicians for Canada, Japan, and South America, and also served as a *peritus* [theological advisor] during the Second Vatican Council. In 1969 he was consecrated a bishop, and in 1972 was called to Rome where he was named Rector of the Pontifical Canadian College.

As a papal secretary, Mario Marini came to know Archbishop Gagnon when seeking legal advice on certain matters for the Holy See. Suffice it to say, Marini was duly impressed with Gagnon: his mind, work ethic and no-nonsense professionalism. Knowing the Canadian archbishop's love for Latin America, Marini invited him to the December 12th *fiesta* of Our Lady of Guadalupe at Pontifical Mexican College. It was then and there, between *Son de la Negra* and *Volver, Volver,* that Don Mario Marini introduced Archbishop Édouard Gagnon to the mariachis' sole *gringo* and second-trumpet: me.

Gagnon was fluent in seven languages and spoke them all with a beautiful yet decidedly French accent. When the two of us were together, we usually spoke English with a smattering of French; when Mario was with us, it was Spanish with a smattering of everything else.

One evening in 1977, over a plate of *carbonara* in the far back corner table at *Polese's*, Mario and I learned from a visibly shaken Gagnon that his rooms in the Canadian College and his office in San Calisto had been broken into and ransacked. He added an even more shocking revelation: "Last night," he said quietly, "I received another death threat — the second in two months."

"Phoned, or written?" Mario asked automatically.

"Written," answered Gagnon.

"You called the police, no?" I inquired.

Gagnon dismissively shook his head in the negative.

"Charlie, Charlie," Marini rebuked, "Involve the civil authorities? Call in the clowns? For so serious a matter? Never."

Edouard Cardinal Gagnon

Édouard Gagnon then proceeded to address the more specific reason he asked us to dinner.

He wondered if it wouldn't be better for the delicate mission entrusted to him by the pope - to say nothing of his own physical safety — to stay a bit closer to trustworthy friends, i.e., Mario and me. Naturally, both of us encouraged him to do just that. Archbishop Gagnon took the last room available on our floor in the Lebanese Residence. I spent the following Saturday driving his brown Fiat back and forth between the Canadian College and our place, carting boxes of books, clothing, and photographs —and several sealed boxes of documents.

Now, by no means did the good archbishop entertain the notion that Mario Marini and Charles Murr would make a fine pair of bodyguards in an emergency. While his change of address had much to do with friendship and the trust he had in Mario and me, Édouard Gagnon was far too pragmatic to rely on us for physical protection.

As I say, Archbishop Gagnon was a pragmatist.

You see, our house, the Lebanese Residence, had recently received another resident: another archbishop, in fact. After two and a half years of Vatican/Israeli negotiations, fifty-five-year-old Hilarion George Capucci, Melkite Archbishop of Jerusalem-In-Exile, had just been released from an Israeli maximum-security prison. He had served two years of a twelve-year sentence for smuggling weapons to the PLO [Palestinian Liberation Organization] on the West Bank. The Syrian archbishop's room was at the one end of the third-floor corridor, mine was at the opposite end of the same corridor, and Marini and (now) Gagnon had the two center rooms.

Why was this the ideal "safe house" for Archbishop Gagnon? And why did he need protection in the first place? As to the former: given Archbishop Capucci's unique situation, directly outside our building were parked two vans and a Mercedes-Benz sedan —each occupied by men armed and ready for action, 24/7. The first van belonged to the Syrian Secret Police, the second van to the Israeli Mossad, and the sedan to the Italian SISMI [Military Intelligence Agency]. They did nothing but watch *Via Fratelli Bandiera*, 19 -- *and* each other. Though each organization had its own reasons for being there, all three had their focus on one man: Archbishop Hilarion George Capucci.

But why did this Canadian archbishop need protection?

Why had his rooms been ransacked and his life threatened? This brings us to the center of our drama, and it is essential for me to provide some historical background.

On the Solemnity of Saints Peter and Paul, June 29, 1972, in the Basilica of Saint Peter, His Holiness, Pope Paul VI delivered a sermon that immediately captured the attention of millions throughout the world, Catholic and non-Catholic alike. Lamenting the chaotic state of the post-Vatican II Church, the pontiff declared: "Through some fissure, the smoke of Satan has entered the Temple of God."

A couple of years later, two highly-respected Cardinals of the Roman Catholic Church — Cardinal Dino Staffa, Prefect of the Apostolic Signatura [the Supreme Court of the Catholic Church] and Cardinal Silvio Oddi— met privately with Pope Paul and placed before him documentation of a very damning nature — documentation indicating exactly where in the temple wall His Holiness might find that fissure.

The damning documents concerned two high-ranking members of the Roman Curia: Cardinal Sebastiano Baggio, Prefect of the Sacred Congregation for Bishops, and Bishop Annibale Bugnini, Deputy-Secretary of the Sacred Congregation for Divine Worship. With proof in hand, Staffa and Oddi formally accused Baggio and Bugnini of being active Freemasons and, as such, traitorous infiltrators of the central government of the Roman Catholic Church. The seriousness of the matter could not be greater, given the positions these men held.

Cardinal Sebastiano Baggio, Prefect of the Sacred Congregation for Bishops since 1973, decided who would and who would not become a bishop of the Roman Catholic Church. He chose these episcopal candidates from a pool of half a million priests throughout the world. As the successors of the Apostles, bishops are absolutely essential to the existence of the Church. If, as Staffa and Oddi alleged,

Sebastiano Baggio was the "Freemason Ambassador to the Holy See," the havoc he was in a position to wreak upon the universal Church could cause irreparable damage. The bishops who had been nominated on his watch reflected Baggio's own liberal ideological views. In the view of Staffa and Oddi, and some others in the Roman Curia, the "Baggio Boys" were self-styled "progressives" who were opposed to the central authority of Rome, all too ready to jettison theological orthodoxy in the name of *"aggiornamento"* and "dialogue" with the world. They argued that this trend was supported by the values of the creed of Freemasonry that Cardinal Baggio covertly espoused.

As for Bishop Annibale Bugnini, Secretary of the Congregation for Divine Worship and undersecretary in the Congregation for Rites, his Freemason attachment, if true, could explain the radical liturgical revolution taking place in the Catholic Church. The implementation of the directives of the Second Vatican Council had patently gone far beyond the stated intentions of the Council Fathers, and indeed at times actually contradicted them. Venerable rites, customs, and devotional practices that had been safeguarded and passed on for centuries were simply swept aside. Several members of the committees formed under Archbishop Bugnini, who had served as experts during the Council, came to regret and repent of their involvement in the work of liturgical reform. As he watched the machinations of Archbishop Bugnini, one of these theologians, Father Louis Bouyer, came to the conclusion that the man was "as bereft of culture as he was of basic honesty." Annibale Bugnini's Masonic membership could certainly explain much that was going drastically wrong in the Church, liturgically, doctrinally, and morally.

Cardinals Dino Staffa and Silvio Oddi urged the Holy Father to bypass his Secretary of State, the Frenchman Cardinal Jean Villot, when dealing with this matter because they believed his ties with the accused, and in particular with Cardinal Sebastiano Baggio, were too close for comfort. At their behest the Holy Father turned this sensitive and potentially explosive situation over to the one man who enjoyed his complete trust: Archbishop Giovanni Benelli.

By papal mandate, at once, the Vatican Deputy Secretary of State, Giovanni Benelli, set out to double- and triple-check the authenticity of the documents; to verify them and verify them again. The pope met with Archbishop Benelli and they agreed that nothing was to be said about these grievous accusations to the Secretary of State, Cardinal Villot, until the right investigator could be identified and an official announcement of the investigation be made.

"Then, be very quick about it," Papa Montini directed. And he urged that the matter be kept extremely confidential.

"Certainly, I share your desire for secrecy on this entire matter," Benelli declared, "however, how can it be successfully executed in absolute secrecy? I will need help with this. There are two men in the Secretariat who have shown themselves trustworthy. I ask your permission to enlist their assistance in this, Holy Father."

Out of curiosity, not mistrust, the pontiff asked: "Do I know them?"

"Archbishop Donato Squicciarini," he answered, "and our Ravenna Engineer," he said, referring to the longtime beneficiary of the pope's beneficence, "Mario Marini."

It took Giovanni Benelli months to uncover what his investigation called for, but through vast international diplomatic networking and after extensive examination of the evidence, he knew much more about Baggio and Bugnini than he cared to know, and more about the two than they themselves did. He had more than sufficient evidence of Baggio and Bugnini's membership in French and Italian Freemasonry. When Benelli reported back to Pope Paul, he assured him that, although Baggio and

Bugnini were the *"pezzi grossi" [heavyweights]* in this Vatican scandal, they were only *"la punta dell'iceberg" [the tip of the iceberg]*, an image the Italian archbishop had picked up while serving at the Nunciature in Ireland.

Pope Paul VI and his Deputy Secretary met alone in the papal apartment. As Benelli feared, after he demonstrated his findings to the Holy Father and explained them at length, the pope did not say a word. The look on his tired face was one of confused concern. If he was disinclined to speak about the results, thought Benelli, how much more reluctant would he be to act? Nonetheless, knowing his boss better than anyone else in the world, Giovanni Benelli anticipated this very reaction and broke the silence with a sweeping proposal.

"What this calls for, Holy Father," he began forcefully, "is an in-depth and official investigation. An impartial, independent, far-reaching, thorough investigation — one that does not involve me at all. There's reason to believe that Vatican finances are also in jeopardy. No, Holy Father," Benelli said more vigorously, "this calls for a top to bottom, bottom to top inquiry," he said and looked the pope squarely in the eyes, "A visitation," he announced, "A Canonical Visitation of the entire Roman Curia. Yes," he said, with a very Roman shrug of the shoulders, the palms of his hands outward and upward, "No doubt, this will take time and great competency to complete… perhaps a year or two," he said, certain that the more time added to the equation, the more at ease it would put the pope. No "decisive and definitive judgement" was being asked of him — not just yet, at any rate.

"If Your Holiness agrees," Benelli pushed forward, "I have just the man for the assignment. Fit and able." *"Poverello [The poor man],"* the pontiff sighed softly, already feeling sorry for whoever it was Benelli had in mind, "And who might this unfortunate fellow be?" the Holy Father

asked with a look of concern, as he pushed back his chair
and slowly rose to his feet.

Giovanni Benelli also stood, turned his head quickly
from side to side, and straightened up. He cleared his
throat, then spoke: "A French-Canadian canon lawyer
and theologian," he said, "I am impressed by the man's
integrity, his intelligence and his faith. Archbishop
Édouard Gagnon, Holy Father. Rector of the Canadian
College. We have solicited his legal opinions on various
questions and his responses have always been clear, exact
and correct. Gagnon is true believer in God and a loyal son
of the Church."

"Fit and able..." the Pope muttered to himself and
mused momentarily over his friend's recommendation, "...
If you also find him *willing,* Giovanni, then let him begin,"
the old man concluded, and turned toward the tall oak
door to leave for his chapel.

A MIGHTY OAK FELLED

February 10, 1978

Both hands resting atop the low enclosure wall, seventy-three-year-old Jean Cardinal Villot stood staring at some fixed point on the campanile's sooty façade. He took in an extra deep breath of the cool early afternoon air. It was one o'clock, Friday, the tenth day of February, 1978; two days into Lent, with a gray and heavy atmosphere to match both the liturgical season and the cardinal's sour mood. He left the terrace and headed for his office, smiling slightly to two men and a woman seated uncomfortably in the cramped waiting room. With a slight nod to the uniformed porter who rose dutifully the moment the tall Frenchman reentered the secretariat from his cigarette break, Villot started down the narrow hallway and told the young priest, his diplomat-in-training secretary, to call in the last appointment of the day.

Jean Cardinal Villot took his seat at the desk and waited impatiently. More than enough time had passed, Villot assured himself: nearly ten months, now, since he was freed from the obnoxious proximity of his personal nemesis; ten months since Giovanni Benelli had the pope promote him to be Archbishop of Florence and then, in record time, convinced the pope to name him a cardinal! Well, *promoveatur ut amoveatur* — the silver lining to this particular cloud was that Cardinal Giovanni Benelli had been "kicked upstairs" and was now far away from the Secretariat of State and the Holy See.

Yes, it was time. High time… Just a few more minutes and it would be over. Villot looked at the clock on his desk. One-fifteen. Where was the man? Was he making him wait on purpose? Did he suspect this was about to happen? No. Nonsense. How could he? Besides, the Secretary of State had not said a word to anyone — except to Casaroli, and if there were two areas in which Agostino Casaroli excelled, they were in never thinking for himself and always keeping his mouth shut. Golden attributes in the diplomatic world! Jean Villot found these, coupled with Casaroli's own jealousy of Benelli, reason enough to give him Benelli's old job as Deputy Secretary of State.

Where was he? There were less than ten minutes before quitting time.

Benelli had been a long thorn in Villot's side for all those years they were forced to work together. But now, as a cardinal, the *Tuscano* would not only be a major player in the next papal election, he would be his principal adversary. Not that Villot entertained any illusions of becoming the next pope himself. No, his fear was that Benelli might be elected. In any event, the time had come to settle a few old accounts, one with a remote cause four years old.

Where was he? Where was Giovanni Benelli's personal spy in the Secretariat of State?

The proximate cause for score settling was the mysterious Apostolic Visitation of the Roman Curia that had been going on now for two years. This secret investigation — planned and executed independently of the Secretary of State himself! — was under the sole direction of Benelli's handpicked and papally-appointed Archbishop Édouard Gagnon. And presently, the French-Canadian's explorations had brought him dangerously close to Villot's closest Vatican ally, the man he had fought hard to be named Prefect of the Congregation for Bishops: Cardinal Sebastiano Baggio.

No one doubted that somewhere inside Édouard Gagnon's reportedly monumental collection of files lay the reason for Bishop Annibale Bugnini's shockingly swift removal from the Congregation for Divine Worship and

Jean-Marie Cardinal Villot

his "promotion" to Iran as nuncio. By now, everyone in ecclesiastical Rome had heard the scathing claim of Bugnini's membership in Italian Freemasonry.

But the straw that broke the Cardinal Secretary of State's back was yesterday's disturbing report regarding a dangerous move —both literally and figuratively— by Archbishop Édouard Gagnon. Villot was seated at his long desk in the conference room when Monsignor Franco Croci entered with the news.

"He left the Canadian College," Croci informed his anxious superior, and then whispered: "They say his rooms there had been broken into," and raised his eyebrows.

"Yes, yes," Villot snapped, "Tell me something I don't know."

"Yes," the monsignor answered, "but — and I think Your Eminence will find this most interesting - His Excellency, Bishop Gagnon now resides at number nineteen, *Via Fratelli Bandiera.*"

"And I should find that interesting, because …?" Villot asked as he lit another stinking *Gauloise* and inhaled deeply.

"Well …," Croci continued slowly, "It seems that the 'Visiting Inquisitor' has taken the room right next door to our very own Don Mario Marini!"

That was it!

What more proof did Villot need? With Benelli no longer there to protect Marini, he would rid himself of the traitor with one swift blow to the neck. And, through Croci and a few others like him, he would get the word out to every curial cleric who valued his career to avoid their former colleague like the plague.

Mario Marini arrived and entered, but Cardinal Villot did not invite him to be seated. Instead, swiftly and most unceremoniously, he dismissed him from the Secretariat of State and declared him *persona non grata* in Vatican City. As none was technically required, he was given no reason for his dismissal. The news fell on Mario's head and broad shoulders like a virtual ton of Roman bricks and, before he could catch his breath, Villot presented the now former *minutante* with a prepared statement declaring that he accepted the Holy See's decision to terminate his services without protest.

"I remind you of your oath of obedience to our Holy

Father, the pope, and to the Holy See," Villot stated. "It is the Holy Father himself who demands this of you. His Holiness wishes your departure to be an amicable one."

With his head spinning from the shock of the *coup de grâce* and the brutal briskness of its execution, Mario Marini, pen in hand, leaned over and obligingly affixed his name to the paper. Then, without a word, he walked back to his desk. In a mental fog he gathered up his belongings, knowing that he would not be given a second chance to retrieve anything left behind. Now, in a near complete confusion, somehow the shaken priest managed to make it to the *Cortile del Belvedere*, get into his Fiat, and exit Vatican City through the *Porta Santa Anna*. How he got home without having an accident will always remain a mystery to me.

From my corner reading chair, half way through Nedoncelle's, *La Souffrance,* I heard the Fiat pulling up beneath my window, and then the loud manual pull on the emergency handbrake, Mario's signature move. Two minutes later, Mario himself was standing front and center in my room, having entered without the customary preliminary knock on the door. He stood there, pale and speechless. There was a lost look in his eyes that I had never before seen.

"Good God, man! You look like you you've seen a ghost!" I exclaimed.

"I think I have," he muttered, "My own."

He let his stuffed leather book bag and box of papers drop from his arms onto my bed.

I rose to my feet at once, pulled up a chair for him and, though it was the middle of the day, reached behind my set of the *Summa Theologica*. I had no idea what had happened to him, of course, but I knew enough to bring out the bottle of *Vecchia Romagna*. He remained silent as I poured two short glasses of the *Etichetta Nera*.

Mario downed the drink in one swift swallow — yet another first for me to see. I offered a second shot but he refused.

"I just put in my last day at the Vatican," he muttered.

"What are you talking about?" I raised my voice and tone, unsure I heard him correctly.

He spoke slowly. I listened carefully, taking in each and every word, trying not to show my own deep shock as I beheld, for the first time ever, the solid fortress of my friend reduced to a defenseless wreck of a man. I occasionally interjected a question to keep him from going off track.

From boyhood, I have been at my best in an emergency. The first to push onlookers at the scene of an accident to one side so I could step into the middle of a crisis and do something about it; the one to break up fights; to remove his shirt and bandage a wounded head while others just looked on. I was alert to the bugle call. And here was my friend in urgent need of first aid!

"And Benelli?" I inquired firmly, "Benelli will know what to do... You haven't spoken to him yet, have you? No!" I changed my mind midstream, "On second thought: we do nothing until Gagnon gets home. That's right," I affirmed, "We'll wait for Gagnon. He's a friend *and* a lawyer! He'll know what to do..."

"Yes," Mario muttered, "Gagnon will know."

"My gut feeling, Mario, is that this has a hell of a lot more to do with Benelli and with Gagnon's investigation than it has to do with you — with you personally. Am I wrong?"

"No, no," Mario finally piped up, and with some spitfire back in him, "You're not wrong. That wretched man has always hated Benelli; he hates him even more now that he's a cardinal — a cardinal *and* in the running for pope... He hated me the moment Benelli introduced me to him."

"Good," I was temporarily satisfied, "Then you and I

will wait for Gagnon to come home. We'll talk things over with him. Let Gagnon be your first line of defense. He'll probably tell you to talk with Benelli. But we'll wait for Gagnon. Wait and see."

"You're right," he said already slightly encouraged.

"And try not to be surprised when Benelli isn't," I added.

"What? What was that?" he asked with a very confused look.

"I say: try not to be surprised when you discover that Benelli isn't surprised by what happened to you today." I clarified, "I mean, nothing of any significance happens in Rome without Benelli knowing it. It doesn't matter whatsoever that he's in Florence. Doesn't matter one bit! Benelli could be on the moon; his ears and eyes would still be on Rome. He's got to know by now," I checked my watch, "about what happened between you and Villot, that is."

"Of course," Mario tried to be positive, "He has to know by now," he agreed.

Again, he began to mention some details from the horrible meeting he had had with his former boss when the buzzer in his room next door sounded. He got up at once and walked directly to the phone booth at the end of the hall to answer the call.

When he returned, ten minutes later, it was with the first glimmer of hope that I had seen in his eyes that dreadful afternoon.

"Benelli," he blurted out in the deep bass voice, "He wants me to drive to Florence and see him."

"Fantastic! When?" I asked excitedly.

"I leave tomorrow morning."

"Excellent!" I exclaimed, "That's excellent!" I congratulated him.

I thought Cardinal Benelli's would be the first in a series of phone calls offering my friend help and support, but it was in fact the last phone call. Not even Donato Squicciarini phoned.

However, an hour or so after the Benelli call, I heard a commotion on the street below and went to the window. It was Monsignor Guglielmo Zannoni trying to reach the gate. He had shown up in person without having phoned first. I called to him from the window, and after he got the "once over" by the Italian "FBI" on "Capucci-Patrol," the stocky seventyish Zannoni — spectacles, threadbare cassock and all— was found "unthreatening enough" to enter our modern-day Middle Eastern citadel. Once inside the lobby, I was there to meet him. He was obviously shaken from the security ambush. "Great!" I thought to myself: "One man in need of sedatives, upstairs; another one, downstairs!" At any rate, I did my best to calm him down and, in capsule form, attempted to explain the unusual front gate circumstances.

"From the moment Archbishop Capucci arrived, anyone unknown to the Israelis, the Syrians, or the Italian FBI —all of whom are parked very un-inconspicuously right outside our gate," I stated with as much chagrin as I could muster, "is frisked and interrogated before he's permitted to enter the sacred precincts within." I then accompanied our surprise guest to the elevator.

Monsignor Guglielmo Zannoni was the embodiment of humility and kindness. Half his monthly salary went to the poor. No coins dropped into a poor-box; no cheques to some benevolent institution; Zannoni went personally to visit the poor and the sick. He handed sealed envelopes to those unable to put bread on the table or to meet that month's rent. I had learned all of this from Marina Colonna, owner of *Bar/Café Sant'Ufficio,* a stone's throw from where I worked at the *Ufficio Informazione.* As tough as she appeared on the outside, Marina had a heart of butter.

Quietly, she too helped a number of Rome's unfortunates, especially elderly and lone survivors of World War II. One of her oldsters told her of Monsignor Zannoni's monthly charity runs.

As much as I loved and respected -- and owed -- Mario Marini, I also had a rather eclectic collection of friends I counted on for advice: Pascalina Lehnert, the wise old Bavarian nun; Enzo Samaritani, the married-with-children Roman sophisticate; Édouard Gagnon, the scholarly and courageous; Guglielmo Zannoni, the humble and saintly. Yes, I had friends my own age as well, but they never seemed as interesting to me as my older friends. Nor could I speak as freely with any of them — in fact, I couldn't speak with any of them about the most things important in my world, delicate matters that I'd promised Mario, Gagnon, Zannoni and Squicciarini to keep absolutely to myself.

When, finally, the elevator showed up and we arrived outside Mario's room, I left Zannoni and him alone to talk out the disastrous happenings of the day. Half an hour later, two solid bangs on the wall told me I was invited to join them.

"Of course," Zannoni hesitated, when I walked in, and then got an OK-nod from Mario to continue, "as I was telling Don Mario," he cleared his throat, "...certainly, the personal antipathy between Cardinal Villot and Cardinal Benelli explains what happened today. Cardinal Villot takes Don Mario for a, well, for a Benelli emissary."

"A Benelli *emissary?*" I questioned the word usage.

"A spy," Mario clarified.

"Yes," Zannoni concurred, "A 'spy,' if you will... His Eminence feels freer to act without you and me there to take note." He turned and looked at Marini.

"Tell Charlie what Villot did to *you*," Mario coaxed him.

"The appointment?"

"To the Congregation for the Clergy," Mario completed it for him, "Yes, exactly. Just last year."

"What is there to tell?" Zannoni asked rhetorically, "I was asked to leave my post..."

"Head of personnel for the Vatican Secretariat of State, no less," Marini interjected.

"Yes," continued Zannoni, "in the Secretariat of State, and accept the position of Deputy-Secretary to Cardinal Wright, your compatriot," he looked at me and smiled, "A very good man, Cardinal Wright. Clear-thinking, *pragmatico*..."

"Without letting Benelli, his Deputy-secretary, know a thing about the 'promotion,'" Mario emphasized, "So the good *Monsignore*, here," Mario continued, "an eminent canonist and one of the finest Latinists in the world, head of personnel for the entire Secretariat of State, was relieved of his responsibilities in the Secretariat to serve as assistant to an American cardinal."

"But you forget," Zannoni offered, "it was with Cardinal Benelli's knowledge and final approval."

"And *you* forget," Mario went on, "that Benelli discussed it with you beforehand — and had you not agreed to the transfer he would have fought for you to stay right where you were."

"Don Mario," he said and lowered his head, "from the beginning, I go where I am sent."

"All I'm saying is that it's one thing to say he knew, it's another to say he approved." Mario corrected, "There's no way Benelli *approved* of what Villot did to you — when Villot finally got around to telling him, *Monsignore*." Mario disagreed with his guest's overly charitable interpretation of last year's maneuverings, "Villot sent you to the Congregation for the Clergy because he considered you an ally of Benelli. And because he had the upper hand just then."

"The upper hand," I repeated, "What do you mean by that?"

"He knew Benelli wanted Florence and the red hat. And it was obvious that Benelli had arranged that, privately, with the Holy Father. Pope Paul saw the writing on the wall," he simply affirmed the inevitable, "and gave his blessing to it."

"And, oh, how it must have pained him —to resign himself to live the rest of his days without Benelli, his trusted friend!" Zannoni's somewhat lachrymose lament sounded like an exclamation from a Greek chorus.

"It was either that," Mario jumped back in, "or leave Benelli to be torn apart and devoured by ravenous hyenas the second after he breathed his last!"

"God forbid," Zannoni said under his breath.

"And Villot knew that Benelli wouldn't do anything that might ruin his chances for Florence. No, Villot is bent on ridding the Secretary of State of anything related to Benelli! Yesterday, it was you," he told Zannoni, "today it is me."

It was completely unlike Mario Marini to feel sorry for himself like this. It unnerved me to see him so deeply wounded and it unsettled me to see him so vulnerable. Yet, I couldn't blame him. The world, his world, had been pulled out from under him and he was flat on his back with all the wind knocked out of him. But, seeing how and where Mario was at this moment, my personal question was: how and where was I in all this? He needed me strong and reassuring right now. I put on my most confident face for him —and for myself.

"Well…, I understand your anger and your pain," Zannoni said and closed his eyes very tightly for a moment, "…And I understand how the injustice of the dismissal makes you want to lash out," he went on, "But, I'm afraid this battle —and I do not minimize it, *caro* Mario, not at all

Monsignor Guglielmo Zannoni

— but I'm afraid that the injustice foisted upon you today is blinding you to the much greater war going on," he said, "Now, in these very days, the future of the Church herself hangs in the balance."

"The next conclave?" I was impertinent enough to mention it by name, "Is that what you mean?"

"Could there be anything more crucial?" the Monsignor answered my question with his own, "Anything more vital to the Church at this time in history than the conclave that elects the next pope?" he asked me. Then, after taking a moment to weigh his words, he turned to Mario: "Obviously, the cardinal-electors must select the right man, a man of God, with fortitude and courage, to lead God's Church out of this — this — out of this *ungodly* state of chaos," he took a deep breath, "This weighs on Benelli heavily, day and night." He addressed Mario, "We all know that the outcome of the next conclave is all-important to the future of the Church… What happened to you today, Mario, was a sword to the heart," (I had never heard him called Mario Marini by his first name before today), "but you, more than anyone, know that this is about so very much more than you. Cardinal Villot would like nothing better than for Benelli to come running to your rescue — so he could accuse him of meddling in the internal affairs of the Secretariat of State. You know how a perverse mind can twist and manipulate such things to its own advantage… You mustn't let Cardinal Benelli get burned trying to help you. Not now. Not this close to the next conclave."

"Do you think I don't know that?" Mario retorted with respectful restrain, "But I've got to say, my friend, that right now, with all that's happened to me today, the last thing on my mind is the next papal election."

"Then I suggest you reprioritize," said Zannoni with more force and determination than I had ever heard in him. "Do not ask Benelli to do anything that, at this critical time, would put him in direct conflict with the Secretary of State … not to mention a conflict with Cardinal Baggio."

"O-o-o-o-o," moaned Marini, "Imagine the triumphant joy in that black heart today! Baggio had his fat hand in this, too; Villot *and* Baggio! I've been in that Judas's crosshairs for years — the Masonic traitor… I'll get Giuseppe Lobina on the case," he said, like a man grasping at straws, "He's one of the best lawyers in Rome."

Zannoni shot Mario a reproving glance.

"It's all right;" Marini responded to his look, as if to say: Charlie knows.

And what I knew was precisely what the two men seated before me knew; what Cardinals Giovanni Benelli, Silvio Oddi, and Pericles Felici knew. I knew what the former Prefect of the Apostolic Signatura, Cardinal Dino Staffa, knew (and who, weeks prior to his recent demise, had turned over to Édouard Gagnon every piece of evidence he had concerning the Bugnini and Baggio Freemason matter). And, naturally, I knew what Cardinals Baggio and Villot knew; and what the recently-appointed Nuncio to Iran, Bishop Annibale Bugnini knew. I knew it all, all too well.

Seeing Mario so upset, so out of sorts, so *not* himself, caused me to speak boldly: "I say: make no decision, and take no action whatsoever, until Gagnon gets home. With all due respect, Monsignor Zannoni," I turned to him directly, "I suggest you and I leave Don Mario alone right now," then, turning directly to Mario Marini, "and that you lie down, put your feet up, and *try* to rest. As for me, I'd love to give our good and loyal friend, Monsignor Zannoni, a ride home - and on my way back," again I looked at Mario, "I'll stop and get you something to eat. That's what I say," I added emphatically.

Unbelievably, my voice, the voice of reason, registered with my audience of two.

No sooner had I returned from taking Zannoni home and delivered a specially-made *calzone* and small bottle of Montepulciano to Mario Marini, when I heard agitated noises from the street below. Once again, Archbishop Gagnon was desperately attempting the impossible: fitting his sizeable Fiat Mirafior into a parking place designed for a Fiat 500. I hurried down to help him park and manage whatever he had to carry in. There was always a box of something. Of course, first and foremost on my mind was to tell him the news about Mario.

Today, the 58-year-old Canadian looked particularly fatigued; not worn out, but certainly worn down. Even his glasses looked wrong for his normally full and strong face; they rested too low on his nose. Édouard Gagnon had spent the entire afternoon at San Calixto in Trastevere. Before I could say a word about Mario, he began airing a few complaints about his own day: "...interviewing people who asked me not to meet with them in their own Vatican offices. Even inside San Calixto, some asked to speak with me on the terrace, others in the garden — one even asked to be interviewed in the parking lot. What a day," he groaned quietly and concluded with one of his favorite French sayings,"E voilá pourquoi votre fille est muette!"[1]

Then, between the gate and the front door, I blurted it out: "Mario was fired from the Secretariat this morning. Villot dismissed him. No reason given."

Gagnon stopped walking, raised his head, and straightened his back.

"How is he taking it?" he asked me, "I mean, I don't suppose he's taking this laying down."

"Hard," I answered.

"Let's go," he ordered encouragingly, "Has he spoken to Benelli?"

I told Gagnon that, indeed, Benelli had phoned Mario and had invited him to Florence.

"He plans on leaving for Florence in the morning," I reported.

Gagnon and I entered Mario's room and found him at his desk. Worry was written all over his face. He had been writing in a notebook, which he closed as we sat down on the only available chairs.

Rather than listen to the account of the Villot firing for the fourth — or was it the fourteenth? — time, I excused myself, went downstairs to the chapel and offered Mass,

---

1 This is a line from Moliere's *Le Médecin malgré lui*, and literally means: "... And so, THAT'S why your daughter is mute!" It is the conclusion to a very long rigmarole of absurd terminology by Sganarelle, the quack doctor, who pretends to provide a medical diagnosis. Archbishop Gagnon loved to quote the line to express a whole series of events, ending with, "There you have it, and so there you are!"

which I had not yet done due to the unexpected bombshell. When I returned to the third floor, forty minutes later, I was in time to pick up a few straggling details in the Gagnon/ Marini question and answer session.

"Benelli's a kind man," Gagnon was saying, "no doubt about it — but you can be sure that he didn't phone and invite you to Florence as a simple act of kindness. No, he wants to hear exactly what happened between you and Villot. And he wants to hear it straight from *your* lips. It's imperative that you tell him fully and truthfully what transpired — not that you wouldn't tell him the truth," Gagnon shook his head to the negative, "I don't mean that," he sought to clarify, "I mean, weigh your words carefully. You know Benelli's memory. If he needs to quote you — and he *will* — it will be word for word. You know what I'm saying, Mario. You know him better than anyone. It's imperative he hear the whole story," he repeated, "and as soon as possible."

"I leave first thing tomorrow morning!" Mario seemed to protest a bit, as if asking: How much quicker do you want it?!

"God only knows how many versions of it he's already heard," Gagnon sighed as he checked his watch, "And it happened only a few hours ago! Lies and disinformation, they're the enemy's labyrinth."

"*Certo [For sure],*" mumbled Mario.

"May I add just one thing more?" the archbishop asked.

"Certainly."

"I know how upset you are. What they've done to you is diabolical…" he adjusted his glasses, "Just do not be surprised or, for heaven's sake, get angry, when Benelli advises you to be patient and to wait; that there's nothing he can say or do just now. When he tells you that, believe him."

"I don't understand," I added my modest objection, "What do you mean, there's nothing Benelli can do?"

"Not now; not at this point." Édouard Gagnon, pressed his lips together tightly and waited a moment before continuing, "The timing would be terribly wrong."

"That's why Villot waited until now — after Benelli was long gone— to act," Mario explained to me.

"You might be more correct than you know," Gagnon mused. He grinned slightly. "Yesterday I phoned the Secretary of State with an update. My work on the investigation is practically at an end. It just needs to be typed and edited —of course, only I can do the editing." He rolled his eyes and sighed, "There's nothing more to add or subtract. The final draft should be ready to present to the pope next month," he announced to the two of us. "The cardinal seemed very pleased with the news… That's what has me worried."

"I don't understand," I said.

The rather stern expression on Mario's face told me not to interrupt the good man.

"He was too gleeful —too eager to accommodate me — that is, until I qualified my request. I told him that I was asking for a strictly private audience —'private,' as if to say: 'sans Votre Eminence.'"

"You told him that?" I asked incredulously.

"Gne-au-gh!" Gagnon scoffed with a laugh, "Of course not! I told you, 'as if!'" He said this to clarify the matter for the benefit of the naïve one-half of his audience.

"How did he react to that?" Mario asked seriously.

"Displeased. Irritated," Gagnon said and, once again, he grinned slightly.

This major news-flash instantaneously lifted Mario Marini's spirits. (It didn't do me any harm, either!) However, I knew not to push any further; not to ask those questions that both Mario and I were anxious to know the answers to: Were major changes in store for the Roman Curia?

Many Vatican bureaucrats already acclaimed *or* blamed Édouard Gagnon — depending on which side of the Masonic line of demarcation the particular bureaucrat stood — for Bishop Annibale Bugnini's suddenly "promotion" to Iran (and Roman departure). That was two years ago, one year into Gagnon's investigation. With Gagnon's final report soon to be presented to the pope, all sorts of questions filled my head. Would discipline and order be restored in the Church? To her priests? To her religious? In her seminaries? To her schools and universities? Would the ancient liturgy be celebrated once again? Was the nefarious reign of Cardinal Sebastiano Baggio about to end? If so, might Baggio have room in his luggage to take Cardinal Jean Villot with him?!

But our suffering friend had a very personal question he wanted answered: When Gagnon met with the Holy Father, alone, *sans* Villot or anyone else, would he explain his unjust predicament to him? Still, Marini knew better than to ask that of Gagnon right now. He would say or do nothing without first consulting with Benelli… and that would happen in just a matter of hours.

Archbishop Gagnon stood up, assured Mario of his prayers, encouraged him and insisted he not despair. He urged him to continue to be the strong man of unwavering faith he knew him to be. He thought a moment and then asked if he could drop by later with a letter for Mario to deliver to Cardinal Benelli when he saw him?

"Consider it done," Mario Marini loudly agreed.

PURGATORIO IN DANTE'S FLORENCE

February 11, 1978

When Saturday dawned that eleventh day of February, 1978, in spite of the gray skies, the cold, and the rain, hope had a place in the heart of Don Mario Marini. In no time, he was on the A1 (Naples to Milan) Highway; *"L'autostrada del Sole! [The Sunshine Highway!]"* he pronounced its famous nickname aloud. With the back and forth of windshield wipers and the defrost fan set on hi, Mario didn't miss the irony of the name, and for the first time in eighteen hours, almost managed to smile.

After a long night of tossing and turning, of considering things this way and that, of going over a list of the same questions and coming up with the same non-answers, of weighing the possible motives of a hundred possible Judases, he got out of bed at four o'clock, more fatigued than when he retired early the night before. He showered and shaved, dressed, said Mass, finished his second cup of coffee and was off for Florence by five-thirty.

He much preferred arriving in the Tuscan capital a few hours early rather than remaining in bed one more minute. Besides, arriving early would give him extra time for prayer in the *Duomo* — before the invasion of tourists. The extra time would also give him a chance to go over the points he wanted to discuss with his friend and mentor, Giovanni Cardinal Benelli. This luncheon date was crucial.

Having been so unceremoniously dismissed by none other than the Vatican Secretary of State himself, Mario

Marini believed that his only hope for returning to the pope's service and for justice lay with Giovanni Benelli.

All of the sudden, the rain and wind outside on this stormy day combined with an inner sinking feeling in Mario Marini. It was not so much about the public shame of having been dismissed from the Holy See as from the private satisfaction he was providing to enemies. How delighted Baggio and Villot must be! Have they already placed the phone call to Teheran so that Bugnini might join in the merriment? Surely by now Baggio has phoned his nephew and fellow Mason, Mario Pio Gaspari, whom Marini had moved from his prestigious assignment as Nuncio to Mexico to a much less important post in non-Catholic Tokyo?

Finally, he arrived in Florence. He was early and had plenty of free time before he was to meet with Cardinal Benelli. He parked his car and entered the *Duomo* to pray.

Mario took his place in the very last pew of the Castellani Chapel. He had finished his breviary and felt he had gone the extra mile by tolerating, as a personally imposed penance, the hordes of gum-chewing, camera-toting heathens shuffling their way aimlessly through the great cathedral, with its priceless works of art, without a clue about what they were actually seeing. "What does Charlie call them?" he mused, and then remembered: "…'Useless son-of-riches!'" He made an admittedly imperfect Act of Contrition for a few mental wanderings and for several vengeful thoughts that flitted through his mind during his meditation time. He stood, genuflected to the Blessed Sacrament, and commenced the short saunter to *Via San Giovanni* #3.

Just as the bells of the *Duomo* clanged the quarter hour of noon, the ancient door opened wide enough for the elderly porter to see who it was.

"*Buongiorno,*" said the tall priest with the commanding voice, "Don Mario Marini," he introduced himself, "I'm a little early, I know, but I'm expected for twelve-thirty lunch with His Eminence."

"Si, Don Marini," the old man acknowledged him with a smile, "His Eminence expects you. *Prego,"* he said with a slight head bow and opened the door more fully.

He showed Mario to a tastefully elegant waiting room and invited him to take a seat, which he did. Mario had hardly sat down when he heard two rapid and very familiar-sounding knuckle-knocks on solid oak. The door opened and, with outstretched arms, Cardinal Giovanni Benelli entered and walked straight to his guest. He put both hands on Mario's broad shoulders and welcomed him with the two kisses, left cheek, then right. "Mario... Mario," he called him by his first name, *"Benvenuto, amico mio... fratello mio; benvenuto!"* [Welcome, my friend, my brother; welcome!]

If Don Mario Marini ever cried in his entire adult life, no one ever saw it, nor would he ever admit it. Just now, however, as he closed his tired brown eyes, a small tear from his right eye fell upon his mentor's shoulder.

Giovanni Benelli took a step back to get a good look at his younger friend. It did not surprise him, yet it greatly saddened him, to see the virile, robust man emotionally reduced to a felled red oak.

Mario said nothing for a moment. He couldn't. Then he handed his former boss an envelope. "Archbishop Gagnon, Eminence." The cardinal opened it at once, speed-read it, and put it back inside its envelope.

It might have been his rigorous diplomatic training; perhaps the comfortable freedom that a certain degree of distance between himself and others provided, but as much as he authentically esteemed, admired and trusted Mario Marini, Giovanni Benelli almost always called him by his title, "Don Marini" or "Don Mario" —though recently, and often enough, he would slip and called him by simply by his first name. Nor had he ever given Mario permission *not* to address him by his title. Only two years ago had he invited Mario to address him with the familiar *"tu"* rather than the formal *"Lei."* As far as Giovanni Benelli was concerned, that was close enough. It wasn't that he had no feelings. He did, but they were not on public display.

On the way to the upstairs dining room, Mario's host explained that there would be four other dinner guests who had a previous invitation and whom he could not "uninvite."

"Be just a little more patient," Benelli told him, "We'll have the whole afternoon to talk after they leave."

The dining room was high-ceiling Renaissance at its finest. The only change to it (and the entire house, for that matter) was electricity, some seventy years ago. Those four other guests the cardinal mentioned to Mario on the way to diner included Padre Procopio Pazzi, an elderly Servite hermit, and his benefactor-friends visiting from Pisa, the Fagiolis: Riccardo Fagioli, a rotund, balding middle-aged perfume manufacturer; his extremely talkative wife, Joanna; and their mousey, socially awkward — and, thank God, seemingly mute— twenty-eight-year-old son, Odisseo.

With a profound yet silent inward sigh, Mario Marini took his place at long table. He had been so eager to speak privately with Benelli, and now this. Who were these people? Who cared who they were? And what was he supposed to answer now when asked where he worked, or to which parish he was assigned?

But Cardinal Benelli allayed those worries at once. Immediately after Padre Procopio presented his entourage to him, he introduced his guest to them: "Monsignor Marini and I worked together for years in the Secretariat of State. He's come to see for himself just how I'm faring without his invaluable help," he said and, smiling, turned to Mario, "Ah, for the simpler days of yore! Am I wrong, *Monsignore*?"

"His Eminence is never wrong," Mario answered crisply.

"You can see why I keep him close at hand," the cardinal joked good-naturedly, and then proceeded to bless the table in Latin and invite everyone to be seated.

From that moment on, "Monsignor" Marini had practically nothing to worry about, as *Signora* "Fanny" Fagioli proceeded to talk, almost incessantly and practically without interruption, from *pasta* to *zuppa inglese*. Hers was a nonstop monologue, a virtual travelogue of the recent, five-country, extravaganza tour she had just completed of South America.

As she stopped to inhale, Cardinal Benelli jumped in to ask her husband: "And how did *you* enjoy the excursion, *Signore?*"

"Most unfortunately," Joanna Fagioli had gasped in enough air in time to answer for him, "I had to cancel Riccardo's reservations at the last minute."

"Gli affairi" [Business]," Signore Fagioli raised his head from the plate of *pasta asciutta* long enough to confirm it as his wife dutifully pressed on: Equador, Peru, Bolivia, Chile, Argentina...

"When will it end?" Mario asked himself, "Will it ever?"

Thirty minutes later, as the table was being cleared of plates, Benelli cleared his voice: "Our good Padre Procopio," he began, giving an approving nod to the elderly religious and then fixing his gaze upon Signore and Signora Fagioli, "sings the praises of the Fagioli Family and of your remarkable magnanimity..." In midsentence, Signora Fagioli stopped her monologue and smiled, as humbly as she could manage, to receive the adulation due her, "...and with good reason does he praise you. To sponsor the building repairs and fresco restorations of the Montesenario Sanctuary is a marvelous and monumental commitment that could never be achieved without patrons like you. Without you, *Signore e Signora* Fagioli, precious works of art would be lost to future generations seeking beauty, truth and goodness…"

"The next generation of 'useless sons-of-riches'," Mario Marini thought to himself.

"…Your generosity, Signore Riccardo e Signora Joanna, will be remembered for generations to come. May the Good Lord, in His own time and in His own way, repay your kindness to us, to *La Toscana,* and to the Friar Servants of Mary! Thank you, Padre Procopio, for bringing this fine family here today and for doing us the honor of sharing our daily bread."

The cardinal raised his wine glass and toasted the couple and their son, and in particular the elderly priest.

"Short and sweet," Mario thought to himself and modified Bonaparte to fit the occasion: *"Efficacité, efficacité, toujours efficacité. [Efficiency, efficiency, always efficiency.]"*

With that, however, Padre Procopio —who, thanks to Signora Fagioli, had remained silent throughout the repast— grabbed hold of the table and yanked himself up onto his feet. From the folds of his black habit, like some medieval magician, the old man brought forth several typewritten pages, cocked his head back to better focus through his bifocals, and began: "In the year of Our Lord, fifteen hundred and ninety-eight, the great maestro, Alessandro Allori…

Pie Jesu Domine!! [Kindly Lord Jesus!!] Mario Marini let out a silent scream, fifteen hundred and ninety-eight!! We'll be here until Judgement Day —*the late afternoon of Judgement Day!!"*

He made eye contact with Benelli who, with one microscopic frown, ordered him to endure it all with patience.

Then, out of the clear blue, a miracle! Somewhere in the second half of the seventeenth century, a coughing jag rendered Padre Procopio incapable of continuing one decade further. Down to his toes, Mario Marini felt that his exclamatory prayer had been heard and answered, and peace returned to him — enough of it, at least, to help him smile and bid a cordial adieu to the hermit and the three Fagiolis as the porter reappeared to accompany the four guests back to the main door of the palazzo.

Benelli grinned apologetically at his protégé from Ravenna and, in one three-part sentence, explained the unusual luncheon: "Padre Procopio is a friend of mine; I've known him all my life; a faithful and holy priest." The cardinal then took Mario by the arm and led him to the adjacent parlor for *caffè lungo* and blessed privacy. Mario took a cursory inventory of the room's bluish lace curtains, the half-dead ivy plant on the sill, the grand piano in the corner, and a garish collection of odds and ends, large and small, but shiny-clean.

"*Allora, caro Mario [Well, then, dear Mario];* we've always spoken clearly and directly; man-to-man; friend-to-friend," the cardinal prefaced and went on to say, "I want that same spirit between us, especially now."

"We share a unique history, Eminence, built on trust and, let me say it, our love for the Church. I think we've been honest and frank with each other right from the beginning because we are both believing Catholics and, as such, are not afraid of the truth. In fact, we live for, and serve the Truth."

"*Ben detto [Well said],*" Benelli easily agreed, "Then, suppose you tell me the truth of what occurred between you and the Secretary of State — and by that, Mario, I do not in the least mean to imply that you wouldn't tell me the truth. What I'm asking you to do now is to describe *exactly* what happened. No sentiment, please. Just the cold facts of the matter. We can discuss your interpretation of those facts after we've established what they are."

Now, as always when in Benelli's company, Marini

knew he was in the presence of greatness. No one he had ever known was as intelligent, as methodical, or as razor — sharp and quick as Giovanni Benelli.

As Villot's dismissal of Mario Marini took place within the confines of the Vatican Secretariat and lasted less than ten minutes, there wasn't all that much to tell — nor, for that matter, to have forgotten. Nonetheless, Benelli had him repeat the story, from start to finish, three times, and listened carefully for any added or subtracted details. Marini — who knew how seriously Benelli treated all such matters — coolly performed the triple-recital without altering his volume or tone. The three narrations were pronounced free of alterations, modifications or variations.

Cardinal Giovanni Benelli straightened up in his oversized, overstuffed chair and looked pensively at his former protégé seated across from him on the long sofa. Benelli knew everything he needed to know, and everything his nemesis, Cardinal Jean Villot, intended for him to know.

From his years as Deputy Secretary of State, Giovanni Benelli knew Jean Villot inside and out. He knew that Villot's abhorrence of Marini was an extension of his hatred for him. To attack and humiliate Mario Marini was to attack and humiliate Giovanni Benelli. More alarming, Villot's blatant maltreatment of Marini announced the dire state of health, physical and psychological, of the Holy Father. What happened to Mario Marini could not have happened with the pope's knowledge. Mario was that young man from Ravenna whose progress Paul VI had followed closely from the very beginning; whose years of study, room and board, clothing, even soap and toothpaste, the pope himself paid for, year after year, with his own money; the same exceptional man the pope personally invited to collaborate with him in the Secretariat of State; the same responsible, efficient and intelligent *minutante* the pope inquired about with true paternal concern, when too much time had passed without seeing or hearing from him. No, Cardinal Giovanni Benelli felt it to the bone: things were going from bad to worse in the Vatican. Given its monarchical nature, when a papal administration draws to a close the rats come out of hiding and the vultures begin to circle. Paul VI's reign was nearing its end. The pope's death was nearer than his friend and confidant, Giovanni Benelli, had thought it was; nearer than he cared to think about.

This meant, of course, that the final and very dangerous mêlée was growing closer by the hour. The battle for the Church's future would be colossal and brutal. Either the Church would remain Catholic or — God forbid — be usurped by the likes of Sebastiano Baggio and Jean Villot, and their barbaric band of Masonic sympathizers and Marxists!

Giovanni Benelli understood and was sympathetic to Mario's plight, but he was far more concerned with the impending war for the future of Christianity. He saw in the pained expression on Mario's face that he, too, understood, quite clearly, what was happening; both his own private skirmish and that far greater conflict looming on the ecclesiastical horizon.

"Yet you affixed your signature to this?" Benelli said after reading a copy of the dismissal agreement. "May I ask why?" he inquired with a sour scowl, "Because Villot put it in front of you and said: Sign?" Benelli asked with mounting frustration, "Why would you yield to such a demand? After all your time in the Secretariat?! Did you bother reading it *before* you signed?" he asked with mounting annoyance - though the object of his anger was not Mario Marini, but Cardinal Villot. Before it went any further, Benelli caught himself and, at once, apologized for raising his voice.

A little wounded, Mario said nothing.

The cardinal cleared his voice and looked him eye to eye.

"Don Mario Marini," he began, as a bailiff might summon a first witness to the stand, "Did you affix your name to this sheet of paper *freely?* That is, did you sign it of your own free and complete will, with no one and/or no outside influence impeding your freedom in any way?"

"Well," began Mario Marini, "I -"

"Stop!" Giovanni Benelli ordered with outstretched hand, palm-side toward Mario's face, "I will read aloud the contents of this paper one more time. When I've finished, you will then listen extra carefully to my next question. Do I make myself perfectly clear?"

"Very clear," answered the slightly frazzled priest.

Benelli began reading aloud Mario's copy of the resignation — the very same that Villot had him sign in his presence. He read it slowly, deliberately. Naturally, there was absolutely nothing wrong with the legal contents or language of the document. As every Vatican document is, this one, too, was airtight. Well, seemingly so. But that was not the point.

When the Cardinal had finished reading the document, he asked: "Now: how much time elapsed from the moment His Eminence set this before you, the very first time you laid your eyes on it, and the moment he demanded you sign it?" Benelli asked and then returned to the more fundamental question: "He did 'demand' your signature, did he not? Three separate times, you told me that he 'ordered' you to sign it."

"The Secretary of State *did not ask* me to sign it," Mario spoke without a moment's hesitation, "He *ordered* me to sign."

"Exactly," he affirmed it, "And with whom have you spoken about this?"

"Archbishop Gagnon," he said at once and somewhat

defensively. "When we spoke by phone yesterday you suggested I speak with him."

"Yes, of course. You'd want to speak with Archbishop Gagnon," the cardinal agreed, and, suddenly remembering, reached into his pocket for the letter Mario Marini handed him earlier, "Who else?" he asked.

"Zannoni heard that I'd been dismissed - as I'm sure everyone else in the Vatican has heard by now." Mario said and offered, "Zannoni, good man and friend that he is, showed up at once, in person, at my front door. I couldn't very well not talk ..."

"Monsignor Zannoni is a saint and a scholar," the cardinal interrupted him, "Wise beyond his years. Time and again, he's proven himself the good and faithful friend to both of us," he nodded at Mario, "A great man to have on your side."

"And Murr," Marini added.

"Murr?"

"Don Carlo," Mario said, "Charlie; the American," he said a bit louder, "*Lago di Bracciano*?"

"*Si, si, si,*" quickly Benelli pulled the name from among the thousands in his mental Rolodex, "Yes. He lives with you. And you trust him, no doubt?"

"I do."

"Then insist with him that he says nothing, *that he speaks with no one* about you or your current situation. Tell him your future depends on it — because it does."

"I'll talk with him as soon as I get back."

"And a canon lawyer? Have you someone in mind?"

"I waited to speak with you, first, Eminence. If you think I've got a case..."

"I do," Benelli affirmed.

"Then," Mario shrugged, "Monsignor Lobina? Giuseppe Lobina. Professor of Law at the Lateran University."

"E brusco [He's abrupt]," was the first thing out of the cardinal's mouth, *"rosco, un po' maleducato [crude, a little rude]"* he summed him up quite neatly, "Yes, I know Lobina…" he said more pensively, "He might be just the man for the job… Yes, good. Abrupt, yes; abrupt, crude and rude…" he said, still weighing things in his mind, "… and the man knows the law, inside and out! Abrupt, crude and rude," he repeated the formula, "And isn't that what we're looking for in a lawyer? Of course, it is!"

For his part, Mario Marini was quietly elated to hear his spiritual "Rock of Gibraltar" speaking this way. This was, bar none, the most difficult problem he had ever faced in his adult life. And he wasn't alone; Benelli was speaking in the first-person *plural!* "And isn't that what *we're* looking for?!"

"Eccolo [There you have it!]" he exclaimed, "A hard headed, irreverent, miscreant of a Sardinian lawyer for our shrewdly sophisticated elder brother from Lyons! Yes, of course! Giuseppe Lobina. Contact him and engage him. If he's hesitant to go up against the Vatican Secretary of State, tell him the Archbishop of Florence recommends him and only him for the job. You may also tell him that, *if he judges it wise* —never tell a lawyer or a Sardinian what he should do," Benelli cautioned with a mischievous smirk that both northern Italians understood beyond mere words, "that *if he wishes,"* he repeated, "I will act as your prime character witness; that I was the first to have interviewed and interrogated you on the question of free will, your *complete* free will —or, in your case, the lack of it— in signing Secretary Villot's prepared statement of resignation. Tell him that only one thing can trump the Church herself, and that's a completely free, well-formed, individual conscience."

"I will contact Lobina as soon as I get home," Mario agreed, "Thank you, Eminence. With all my heart, I thank you."

"Dare I ask?" Benelli prefaced, "Funds, my friend?" he asked outright, "How do you stand financially? The truth now, Mario. This is no time for false pride."

Mario Marini was visibly uncomfortable. He was a proud man, and on certain matters very private — this was particularly true when it came to money. "I live from paycheck to paycheck, Eminence. I haven't given much thought to money... Not because it's not an issue. It is. It's just that, having been dismissed, dismissed just like that," he said with a snap of the fingers, "dismissed from the Holy See... Well, the truth is, my head's still spinning. I haven't had time enough or presence of mind enough to deal with anything, let alone money... I'd hate like the devil to have to ask my parents for help. I haven't told them yet... You and the Holy Father know my family situation better than anyone in the world. If it hadn't had been for the pope's generosity and your own, well, I can't imagine where I'd be today... I can only imagine my father's reaction when he learns I've been expelled from the Vatican! *Gesù mio!*" he exclaimed and shot an evocative glance heavenward. "There's a merchant here in Florence. I've known the good man and his kind wife for years. God has been very good to them. Let me see what I can do. But you:" he pointed at Mario, "as soon as you get back to Rome, make an appointment with Lobina. Tell him your situation and insist that his fees and honorarium be those of a true friend and brother priest! Tell him I said so!"

"I will, Eminence."

"And let me know."

"I will."

The cardinal closed his eyes a moment. "May I also give you another piece of advice?"

"I'm thankful for anything you have to tell me."

"Do not leave Rome," Benelli said, as if it were a commandment, "They expect you to leave. They expect you to flee in shame. Do not!" he insisted and slapped the heavy padded arm of his chair. "Stay right where you are… You'll need a job, of course… I can help you out for the time being. You'll keep that to yourself, understand?"

"Thank you. Yes, understood."

"But you'll have to find serious employment. You know, of course, that this matter will take time to resolve."

"How much time?" Mario asked and, attentively, hopefully, listened to the answer.

"You've worked for the Vatican all these years and you ask me, how much time?" he gave a chuckle and shook his head, "Who can say? A year? Two years? Then again," he shrugged, "the world sometimes changes overnight…" he said and remained quiet a moment.

Mario knew what he was thinking: Circumstances certainly could change suddenly — especially with a captain at the helm as frail and sickly as the present pope. Besides Pope Paul VI himself and his personal physician, Renato Buzzonetti, no one knew better than Cardinal Giovanni Benelli just how rapidly the pope's health was declining. They often spoke by phone. The pope's health was such an issue eight months ago that the Holy Father himself decided to call the extraordinary consistory and make Benelli a cardinal. He wanted his longtime and faithful *aide-de-camp,* his closest friend on earth, guaranteed a loud voice and weighty vote in the next papal election - even though that meant living the rest of his days without Benelli's wise counsel and his formidable strength of character to bolster him.

"I wish I could tell you how long this will take to resolve, Don Mario," Cardinal Benelli said sincerely, "The simple truth is that I don't know. No one does. It would be irresponsible of me to pretend I did, and to give you false hope."

"I understand," Mario answered.

The cardinal lifted his head slightly higher. "Now, to practical matters: you'll need a paying job. No doubt, your case is headed for the supreme tribunal of the Church, and as such, a tremendous amount of patience will be required of you. Are you really up to it?"

"I'll find a job," Mario pretended to be sure of himself.

"I was speaking more about patience than employment," the cardinal laughed. "You weren't exactly the most patient man on staff when you worked for me," he said and smiled.

"I'll learn patience," Marini assured him.

"Very well," he smiled and nodded in agreement with Marini's willingness and attitude, "If you are amenable -"

"In all my life, I've never been in a situation to make me more amenable," Mario admitted with sadness.

"*Va bene [All right, then]*." On Monday, Monday morning, I shall place a call to Padre Giacomo Poletti. Director of the Liceo, *L'Instituto Massimiliano Massimo*, in EUR. Good man, Poletti," Benelli went on, "A Jesuit *and* a Catholic," he flashed a derisive grin to Marini, "at least he was when last we spoke. We were students together at the Gregorian," he said and then asked: "Have you ever taught, Don Mario?"

"Theology. For three years, Eminence," he nodded positively, "in Mexico."

"*Madonnina Santa!*" he said with hands together and pointed upwards, "*El Seminario Regional de Chihuahua*," he pronounced the institute's name with *gravitas* and in his best Spanish accent to compensate for the clumsy gaffe.

"*Asi es [There you are]*," Mario commended him.

A knock on the door announced the housekeeper, a fifty-something woman pushing a wooden kitchen cart with a silver tray, an espresso pot, two demitasse cups, sugar, a plate of biscotti, a small bottle of *Centerbe* and two digestif glasses.

"*Grazie, Signora Maria*," the cardinal said with a smile.

"*I biscotti, Eminenza,*" she proudly announced, "*son' freschi, sono!*" [*The biscotti, Your Eminence, they're really fresh!*]

"Yes, thank you," he said again as she left the room and closed the door behind her.

"So, God willing, if everything goes as we have spoken," the cardinal continued, "we'll have solved some immediate problems," he said and, on the fingers of his right hand, starting with his thumb, he began to enumerate them: "First, you must convince Lawyer Lobina to take your case."

"Do I have your explicit permission to tell him that you're willing to be a character witness?" asked Mario Marini.

"Permission? No, no, Don Mario; I *insist* you let him know. If he accepts the case — and he will — speak to him freely about today's conversation between us."

"Thank you, Eminence."

"Secondly," his index finger joined his thumb, "You're to remain right where you are in Rome. And thirdly," his middle finger joined the other two, "if Padre Poletti answers my call, you should have a job and an adequate income. *Molto bene.* Yes, very, very good," Giovanni Benelli smiled with satisfaction.

Mario Marini took in a very deep breath and exhaled slowly. For the first time in twenty-four hours, he felt at ease.

As if reassuring him that all would be well, Giovanni Benelli purposely ceased all discussion of the dismissal matter and spoke with him, instead, about a number of far less important subjects.

Having put his guest well at ease, Cardinal Benelli reopened Archbishop Gagnon's envelope, retrieved the note and gave it a far more cautious second reading.

"This really is a marvelous day!" he exclaimed, "The investigation of the Roman Curia is completed," the cardinal announced to Marini, "Did you know that? Did Archbishop Gagnon tell you?"

"I knew he was very close to finishing."

"Well, he will ask Villot to schedule a private audience for him with the Holy Father. Hopefully, next week. And now the Holy Father will be able to act on the Visitor's recommendations. I won't bother to write him back," he said, "You'll see him tonight, when you get back to Rome, won't you?"

"I hope to," Mario answered.

"Then, please tell him that Benelli says: *Deo gratias!* And now, now that he's finished, let him know that he is free to speak with me about this or anything else in the world, anytime he wishes… *Deo gratias!*" again he said.

Taking two small cards and a pen from his vest pocket, Benelli wrote on the cards.

"One for Gagnon, one for you," he said and handed them both to Marini, "When I am in Florence, you'll find me at this number from eight p.m. to ten p.m. I alone answer this phone."

"I'll give it to him the moment I see him."

When they had finished their coffee, Mario followed the cardinal's lead and stood up to leave.

"…One last word, *caro* Mario," he smiled warmly at his once-and-again protégé: "To endure and complete the journey you're beginning will require a virtue which — and you'll pardon me for saying this - you are not very adept at nor particularly fond of," he said, and patted his friend on the shoulder, "I hinted at it a moment ago. We call this virtue *patience*. Your case will not be resolved in a matter of weeks or months. You know how slowly the Church moves on these matters. To finish victorious will demand the patience of a saint. Learn to be patient, Mario. Patience."

THE FIRST DELIVERY ATTEMPT

May 16, 1978

On an early spring morning, Thursday, March 16, 1978, on *Via Mario Fani*, not far from Sacred Heart University Hospital, a band of Marxist terrorists opened fire on six men in two cars. The Red Brigade terrorists murdered two bodyguards and three policemen who were escorting Aldo Moro to work. Aldo Moro, former Prime Minister of Italy and actual President of the Christian Democratic Party, was kidnapped by the Marxists and held hostage.

To say that Italy, and Rome in particular, was in a prolonged state of chaos and nervous tension would be gross understatement.

And while the seemingly endless tragedy took a tremendous toll on everyone of good will, Italian and non-Italian alike, the horrific kidnapping, murders of five innocent men, and ongoing torture of Aldo Moro most deeply wounded his closest friend in the world: Giovanni Battista Montini, Pope Paul VI.

The pope spent countless hours of his days and nights doing everything possible to negotiate for his friend's freedom. More than once, he offered his own life in exchange for that of his friend's. The offers were soundly and insultingly rejected.

For nearly two months Italy was not Italy, and the normal sweetness of Italian life had turned sour and bitter.

Fifty-four days into the dark national ordeal, Moro's bullet-riddled body was found in the trunk of a Renault

4, on *Via Caetani*, half way between Christian Democratic and Italian Communist Party headquarters in downtown Rome.

The Italian people were in a state of total shock.

The personal toll this took on the Moro Family could never be measured.

Aldo Moro's brutal death hit Pope Paul VI harder than almost anything had ever hit him in life.

Within the Vatican, the word "depression" was a term to be avoided assiduously. Rather, for a period of approximately 143 days —from Moro's abduction to Paul's death— there were some good days among the majority of bad ones —those closest to the Holy Father noted that he was suffering from "melancholia." At times, his audiences, public and private, were cancelled due to a severe lack of energy, chest colds, and the ever-worsening and painful arthrosis. But, worst of all, the pontiff openly and increasingly spoke about death —his own.

It was Tuesday, May 16, 1978.

After three previously-scheduled private audiences between the Roman Pontiff and his Apostolic Visitor had been suddenly cancelled, it was "almost a sure thing," said Deputy Secretary of State Agostino Casaroli in yesterday's phone call to Archbishop Gagnon, "that tomorrow's audience will happen."

Of course, the Deputy apologized profusely for the previous cancellations. That was, after all, part of his job. But, he honestly offered in his own defense, it was beyond his powers to guarantee the Pope's good health and his ability to hold audiences.

At any rate, as of late yesterday evening, Casaroli seemed sure that the Pope was up to receiving Archbishop Édouard Gagnon this morning.

It was nine o'clock and I was growing anxious.

Before I got to the door of the house chapel, I saw a

Giovanni Battista Montini, Pope Paul VI

light on in the sacristy and heard a dresser drawer open and close. I peeked into the sacristy, saw a long black veil, and knew I had the wrong archbishop.

"*Sabah Alkhyr, Siedna [Good morning, Your Excellency],*" I greeted Archbishop Hilarion Capucci in my paltry Arabic, then switched to French, "Have you seen Archbishop Gagnon?"

"I have," said the smiling Syrian, pointing to the next-door chapel.

Faster than you could say *"Shukran"* I was at the chapel door, opened it, and found the Canadian prelate deep in prayer.

I cleared my throat to get his attention and inhaled the air sweet with the scent of frankincense.

"Excellency," I whispered loudly, "I'm in the lobby," and gave the crystal of my wrist watch two quick finger taps, "three past nine," I added respectfully, genuflected, and closed the door behind me.

As uncomfortable as I was interrupting the archbishop's communication with the Lord, I couldn't risk him arriving late for the all-important meeting with the Lord's Vicar on earth!

Walking to the lobby, I thought to myself: "It's here, finally here... The day we've been waiting for since ... since forever! Gagnon's years of work and sleepless nights weren't in vain... Finally, the Church will be purged of the parasites infecting her for decades. She'll have her life back... After the crucifixion, the resurrection!"

I looked through the thick glass in the porter's office at the clock on the wall: seven minutes after nine. While I anxiously checked the clock against my watch, Archbishop Édouard Gagnon and Mario Marini turned the corner and came toward me. Archbishop Gagnon was properly attired for a private papal audience: purple-piped black cassock, silver pectoral cross, purple zucchetto. Mario Marini, also in his clerics and carrying his own black book bag, was on his way to EUR. Thanks to Cardinal Benelli, he was now teaching religion at the Jesuit *Liceo* while waiting for his suit against Cardinal Jean Villot to be taken up by the *Signatura Apostolica,* the Vatican's Supreme Court.

I reached for the black leather book bag Gagnon held by its handles, but he politely rejected my offer to carry it for him. The explosive contents would remain in his custody another fifty minutes, at which time they would be handed over, personally, directly, and exclusively to His Holiness, the pope. He didn't say that. He didn't have to. I read it clearly in the half scowl and pursed lips, and in the curt, "Thank you. No."

"Godspeed, my friend," Marini said as he shook Gagnon's hand, "May your meeting surpass all our expectations."

"God willing," the archbishop responded, "His Holiness will be so motivated as to act, and act swiftly."

"Gentlemen," I interrupted the well-wishing, "if we don't get a move on, no one will be acting one way or the other!"

"Yes," the archbishop agreed.

"*Monsignore*," Mario had a final request, "If the opportunity presents itself…"

"Patience, Mario," Gagnon raised his free hand slightly so that he would not ask what he was about to ask, "There's a time and a place for everything. Today's venue presents neither. Your case is in very competent hands," he said and then added with a bit of justifiable irritation in his tone and look, "You know how crucial today's meeting is to the very life of the Church. To introduce a matter of personal concern, a thing foreign to the discussion, to veer off course even momentarily…" he pursed his thin lips again and shook his head to the negative.

"*Es-tu prêt, Père?*" he looked at me and, curiously, asked in French.

"Am *I* ready?" I questioned the question and exaggerated my expression of surprise.

"*Allons-y alors! [Then, let's get a move on!]* I can't afford to be late today," he added with a small self-deprecating smile.

Nodding a "Good-morning" to the Syrian agents in

the van parked near the house gates [who were watching the Israelis, who were watching Hilarion Capucci and everyone else who entered or exited *Fratelli Bandiera* 19], again I checked my watch. It was nine-sixteen when the archbishop and I were actually seated in his Fiat and ready for take-off. At nine-sixteen and twenty seconds, I hit the pedal and we took off faster than Trastevere pickpockets on a stolen Vespa!

At *Porta San Pancrazio*, Gagnon suggested we pray the rosary for "a successful and productive audience with the Pope," to which I added: "And for smooth-flowing traffic, up to and including the *Cortile San Damaso*." He agreed and took out the beads.

Though the shorter and more direct route to the Vatican entrance at the Holy Office was *Via delle Fornaci*, I decided to tackle the series of sharp and hairpin turns along the less trafficked (at this time of day) *Viale delle Mura Aurelie*. Respectfully, I invited the archbishop to switch his rosary from right to left hand, and to hold tight to the ceiling strap "until we've landed, and the plane has come to a complete stop at the gate."

I followed Gagnon's lead and repeated the prayers with my mouth, but I could not keep my mind from wandering. It wasn't the driving or the road that distracted me, but the realization that I was playing a part, infinitesimal as it may be, in an event of paramount importance: I was driving Archbishop Édouard Gagnon to the most important meeting of his life and, potentially, the most consequential of Pope Paul VI's fifteen-year pontificate.

I knew very well what this morning meant to the great man seated next to me. After years of intense labor, investigations, research, interviews, organizing, and one-on-one encounters with hundreds of people, mostly men, mostly clerics —some, venerable saints and scholars; others, some of the craftiest demons walking the earth— Archbishop Édouard Gagnon now held concrete answers to Pope Paul's enigmatic and disturbing rhetorical question. I glanced over at the strong man; his eyes closed, lost in prayer. I glanced at the briefcase on his lap, knowing it contained the precise ammunition the pontiff commissioned of him. Yes, the unassuming French-Canadian had identified quite a number of those nefarious "cracks in the wall" — the ones through which "the smoke of Satan had entered," and *was continuing to enter,* "the temple of God." Today the historical report on the state of the Catholic Church's central Roman government would be placed before the Holy Father, set squarely upon the desk in his private study, with Archbishop Édouard Gagnon at his side to guide him through the hundreds of pages and answer any questions he may have.

Still, I couldn't shake the feeling that there was something else troubling Édouard Gagnon this morning — something more than the rapidly approaching two-hour meeting with the pontiff.

Never mind the ransacking of his private rooms, the office burglaries, even the death threats. That was in the past. No, it was the present that was troubling Édouard Gagnon. Today's highly anticipated meeting with the pope had taken weeks to schedule; once it had been postponed indefinitely; twice the Secretary of State, Cardinal Jean Villot, cancelled the meeting the day before stating simply that the Holy Father was "indisposed."

Undoubtedly, a significant number of Roman Curia members were dreading today's encounter between the Pontiff and the Canadian Archbishop. Everyone knew about it. No one talked about anything else. I knew that, at this precise moment, any number of people would give everything to have the black leather bag at arm's reach from me thrown into a rip-roaring "bonfire of the atrocities" in Saint Peter's Square, and the ashes strewn into the murky waters of the Tiber! Principal among the very apprehensive men, and the direct cause of a series of delays and postponements of this morning's private audience was none other than the Cardinal Jean Villot.

Three years ago, when the investigation was announced, Secretary of State Villot remarked candidly that such an examination of the Church's central government was a senseless *"chasse aux sorcières"* [witch-hunt], the seeds of which had been planted in the mind of an aged pontiff by *"Le Machiavel Toscan" [The Tuscan Machiavelli,]* then Deputy Secretary of the Vatican State, now Cardinal Archbishop of Florence, Giovanni Benelli.

We had finished the rosary by the time we reached the Holy Office entrance. The Swiss Guards saluted and waved us through. By now (figuratively) half of Rome and (literally) everyone with anything to do with the Vatican knew Archbishop Édouard Gagnon at first sight. As we came around the basilica's apse, moments before entering the archways, Gagnon turned to me: "I know I'm asking a lot, Don Carlo, but could I further impose upon you this morning?"

"Whatever it is, Excellency, consider it done," I answered like a Prussian footman.

"Thank you," he said with a bit of a tired expression on his pale face, "I appreciate all your help. Could you wait for me?"

"Not come back for you at noon?" I questioned, as that was the original plan.

"I'll understand if you can't," he began almost apologetically.

"No, no, no!" I protested, "I just wanted to make sure I understood," I said at once, "Of course I'll wait for you. I'll wait the full two hours — and if he invites you to stay for *pranzo*, know that I'll be right here when you're finished. Don't give it a second thought!"

Another Swiss Guard motioned us to pass under the archway and another still, on the other side of the arch, motioned us into the wide-open courtyard, still wet from the rain but bathed now in morning sunlight.

I pulled up next to the four steps to the elevator, got out of the archbishop's Fiat, went around to open the passenger-door and discovered that, out of nowhere, a young monsignor from the papal household had appeared and beaten me to it.

The tall, elegant priest began to escort the archbishop toward the elevator. By the way Gagnon shook his head, I could see that he absolutely refused to let him carry the leather book bag. Then, suddenly, Gagnon stopped, turned and walked back to me, still standing at the driver's door until he entered the lift.

With what could only be described as a wistful smile, he faced me and whispered: "Pray for me."

"You can count on it, Excellency," I answered, bent and kissed his ring.

For years, as much as Édouard Gagnon looked forward to completing this delicate assignment, he dreaded the thought of this very moment. For an entire lifetime he had done his very best "to judge not lest ye be judged." Yet, in less than twenty minutes, the highest moral authority on earth would bid him act as judge, jury and executioner of a number of priests, bishops, and two of the highest-ranking cardinals in the Sacred College. Nevertheless, it had to be done. And, better than anyone else on earth, Édouard Gagnon knew that if the One, Holy, Catholic and Apostolic Church, founded by Jesus Christ Himself was ever to regain her dignity, strength and true sense of mission, she had to be liberated from some highly placed dignitaries in the Roman Curia.

Why the Lord should choose his shoulders to lay this heavy burden upon was a mystery Édouard Joseph Gagnon would never understand. Yet it was he whom Providence elected, and he was resolved to give Providence his all.

The elevator brought the archbishop and his accompanying monsignor to the top floor of the Apostolic Palace. As the elevator door opened, there, waiting for them, was the gaunt, balding, and bespectacled career diplomat, Archbishop Agostino Casaroli. He had been handpicked by Cardinal Jean Villot to replace the former thorn-in-his-side of a Deputy Secretary of State, now Archbishop of Florence, His Eminence, Cardinal Giovanni Benelli.

Édouard Gagnon was surprised to see Archbishop Casaroli, but he knew to take all the lavished extra attentions as part of the pontifical protocol. Casaroli thanked the young monsignor for accompanying Archbishop Gagnon this far and, with a nod, dismissed him.

"How good it is to see you once again," Casaroli cooed as he escorted Gagnon down the high polished marble corridor, under the tall vaulted ceilings, frescoed by Renaissance masters, that led to the papal apartments.

All of this, everything below him, above him, surrounding him, all of it, was meant to overwhelm and humble the beholder. Yet, today, all of it was wasted on the man from Montreal. He was there strictly on business; not to ponder the glories of the Renaissance, nor to be diverted by choreographed displays of protocol and flattery. No one and no thing would take from the French-Canadian's mind what was permanently filed therein: the complete mental copy of the very documentation dutifully organized and safe within his black leather bag.

They arrived at the final set of double doors in the long corridor. Two Swiss Guards in full dress uniform snapped to attention as Archbishop Casaroli reached for the bronze lever and opened the door.

"*Prego, Eccellenza,*" he said and stepped aside that Gagnon enter first.

At the far end of the long elegant room sat the radiant figure of the Roman Pontiff, His Holiness, Pope Paul VI.

The pope removed his reading glasses with one hand and with the other gestured welcome to his singularly important guest.

Archbishop Édouard Joseph Gagnon's face beamed like the mariner-son returned home from sea and about to embrace his father. He approached the white-robed Vicar of Christ with his gaze so fixed on him that he took no note of the tall lanky figure looming in the shadows. Cardinal-Secretary of State, Jean Villot stood directly beneath the sword that Antoniazzo Romano's brush painted into the hand of the Apostle to the Gentiles. His masterpiece, *The Virgin and Child between Saint Peter and Paul and the Twelve Magistrates of the Rota*, hung high and nobly on the wall behind the pontiff's desk. The Cardinal Secretary of State acknowledged the Archbishop-Apostolic Visitor with a nod but remained silent and stoically stationed at the pope's right hand.

Pope Paul looked pleased to see his specially-appointed Visitor. Édouard Gagnon took the Pope's hand, bowed and in a gesture of obeisance, and kissed the fisherman's ring.

"Welcome, venerable and faithful brother," the Pope greeted him in perfect French.

"Thank you, Most Holy Father, for receiving me. How happy I am to know that you are feeling better," he said, more for the benefit of Villot and Casaroli, who had cancelled and rescheduled this meeting several times in the past two months due, they claimed, to the pope's poor health.

"I wish also to convey my condolences and offer my prayers to Your Holiness for the loss of your beloved friend, Prime Minister Moro."

"We thank you, Excellency," the Pope said quietly and took in an unsteady breath of air, "We appreciate your prayers for his eternal rest, and for the spiritual strength of Aldo's family — Good Lord, what a cross they've been given ...And your prayers for us, Excellency, they are

Virgin and Child by Antoniazzo Romano

needed now more than ever," he said again with a more somber face, a bit shakier voice and, it seemed, the inability to speak for the moment.

While Édouard Gagnon waited respectfully for the pope to regain his composure, he began to think that the good man's bouts with depression were more than cheap Vatican rumor. It became apparent that the kidnapping, torture and execution-style death of his dear friend, Aldo Moro, was the most probable explanation for the cancellation of his three scheduled audiences with Pope Paul.

This insight did nothing to lessen his mistrust of Cardinal Villot or Archbishop Casaroli, but it did help him feel surer of his cause and of himself.

"The years weigh heavy upon us," the pope asserted with mild chagrin, "But, yes, God be thanked, we are feeling better as of late," he smiled, "Please, dear brother, be seated," he said and pointed to the chair on the opposite side of the desk, facing him directly.

Édouard Gagnon took his seat and straightaway placed his black book bag upon his lap.

"It pleases us greatly to learn that you have completed the august assignment we requested of you last year."

The Canadian made no attempt to hide his surprise.

"Begging your pardon," he respectfully interrupted, "It was *three* years ago that Your Holiness assigned me to this investigation."

"*Three* years?"

"Yes, Holy Father."

Visibly perturbed, Cardinal Villot broke his silence: "With so many pressing matters to deal with daily," the Frenchman took a mildly chastising tone, "all of them matters of paramount importance, surely His Excellency can understand how His Holiness could lose track of time."

The Canadian cleared his throat purposefully and then looked intensely into the Pontiff's eyes:

"Holy Father, each of the three times I petitioned the Secretary of State to schedule this 'paramount' and very delicate meeting, I insisted that this initial encounter be between Your Holiness and me. Alone. Private; that we be left alone and able to speak with complete freedom."

Standing slightly behind and to the right of Gagnon, Agostino Casaroli did not take his eyes off the man he hoped one day (very soon) to replace: Jean Villot, who in turn did not take his scrutinizing gaze off Édouard Joseph Gagnon, who, though hearing every word Villot was saying, did not avert his eyes from the pontiff.

"It is the Holy Father's wish," Cardinal Villot assumed the right to inform Gagnon, "that Deputy Casaroli and I be present at this meeting." Villot put a hand on the high-backed chair of the Pope and continued, "Given the extremely delicate nature of the Apostolic Visitation you conducted, and what one might assume to be some extremely delicate findings, today's meeting cannot proceed without witnesses."

The pope was following everything perfectly well and easily detected the tension mounting between Villot and Gagnon, but said nothing.

"When first you asked me to accept this mission, almost three years ago," Gagnon repeated the timeline and, ignoring Villot, continued speaking only to Pope Paul, "I requested complete freedom to conduct the enquiry as I saw fit, *and* that I be answerable to you alone. Your Holiness agreed." Gagnon smiled and gave the pope a small nod of gratitude, "I ask now that the second part of our agreement be honored. I wish to speak with you, and you alone, Holy Father, concerning some," he cleared his throat again, "disturbing 'findings'… After I've explained them to Your Holiness, the course of action you choose will be entirely your own. My work here will be finished. But, before God, I must be sure that you yourself, Holy Father, are made aware of these things; that you hear them from me, clearly and unfiltered, and are free to ask me anything pertaining to them."

Pope Paul VI closed his weary eyes and pinched the bridge of his nose with two fingers. Reopening his eyes, but barely, he turned to his right, to Cardinal Jean Villot and said in an audible whisper: "Leave us, please."

"But Holy Father," Villot protested, "Such official

business — such an audience," he sputtered, "Witnesses — It requires witnesses and assistance..."

"Your generous concern is appreciated," the pontiff answered with restraint, "We will speak with His Excellency as he requested and, as it seems, we agreed. Thank you," he said and turned to look at his fuming Secretary of State, and then to his confused Deputy-Secretary, Agostino Casaroli, still standing next to Gagnon.

Casaroli made a slight head bow. Villot did not. They both walked to the door behind and to the left of the pontiff, the door leading to the Borgia Apartments, and left the great room.

The pope raised his right hand to gesture that his guest should keep silent a moment.

A final click of the door handle, and the much sharper clicking together of guardsman's heels from the other side of the closed door, caused the archbishop to smile a "thank you" to the pope for honoring his "request" so completely.

The pontiff leaned forward and rested both forearms on the desktop. He closed his eyes, then inhaled very deeply and exhaled very slowly before opening them again. He appeared a little more at ease without the cardinal and the archbishop hovering about and peering over his shoulders. At ease, but exhausted.

"*Sans plus tarder [Without further ado],*" Édouard Gagnon said to himself as he set his book bag upon the desk. From it he retrieved one substantial and two smaller tomes: the chronological history of the Visitation, the supplemental documentation to verify the most serious accusations, and a summary of the Apostolic Visitation of the Roman Curia.

"With all respect, Holy Father," Gagnon prefaced his report, "I would not dishonor Cardinal Giovanni Benelli by mentioning him in front of Secretary Villot or Deputy Casaroli, his replacement."

"*Compréhensible,*" [*Understandable*] the Pope answered,

"...*C'est compréhensible,*" he repeated, and immediately stopped the faint curl on his lips from advancing to a smile, "...*On dit que l'envie naît de la peur,*" [*It is said that envy is born of fear*] he said, subtly referring to Villot's long-standing resentment of Benelli.

"Holy Father," Gagnon switched his tone to a more formal one, "the day you summoned me and asked me to accept this assignment, then-Deputy Secretary of State Benelli was also present. That meeting was not just between the two of us, Holy Father, it was actually between the three of us."

"Yes," the Pope remembered.

"I have never spoken with our dear friend, Cardinal Benelli, since he proposed me to you for this very mission. Several weeks ago, I wrote to inform him that the investigation had been concluded, and that I looked forward to delivering the results to Your Holiness.

"I tell you this, Most Holy Father, to assure you that the Visitation was thorough, that confidentiality was of the highest priority, and that I did my best to be fair and impartial from beginning to end.

"Here are the results," he said, turning the thickest volume to face the pope, "along with verifying documentation and a summary of the entire investigation," he concluded as he turned the two smaller files.

Pope Paul put on his reading glasses. He opened the summary volume and scanned the page listing its contents.

"There are many matters that need to be addressed immediately, Holy Father. All of them important; some of them threaten the very life of the Church."

"In your expert opinion, Excellency, which are most urgent? Which is *the* most urgent?" he asked and looked over his glasses awaiting the answer.

"Page four of the summation," he answered at once, "Cardinal Sebastiano Baggio..." he pronounced the name distinctly but quietly. Gagnon drew another deep breath and continued: "…In 1972, Secretary of State, Cardinal Jean Villot," Gagnon also pronounced that name more quietly this time around, "*à lutter farouchement [fought tooth and nail]* for this man - one of his closest friends and political allies - to be named Prefect of the Sacred Congregation for Bishops! Holy Father!" the Canadian archbishop exclaimed and, looking the pontiff straight in the eyes, without uttering one single word, inaudibly shouted the rhetorical: What, in God's name, were you thinking!?

At once, the archbishop knew that this audacious slip of the tongue was a mistake, but today —after three long years holding back his anger over the disastrous state of the One, Holy, Catholic and Apostolic Church - Édouard Gagnon would make known exactly what his investigation revealed and was eating away at him like a cancer.

"A Freemason," Gagnon continued, "A Freemason naming every new bishop in the world! And every new *arch*bishop, given a metropolitan See, and many of them guaranteed a cardinal's hat and a vote in the next papal election! Your Holiness will forgive me for saying this, but a Freemason is orchestrating the next conclave. For all intents and purposes, Cardinal Baggio is naming your successor! And, judging from the lengthy interview he just gave to *Le Monde,*" the archbishop paused a moment to show the pope the correct page in the summary report, "… His Eminence, this same cardinal, is his own favored candidate for pope!"

The pontiff sat upright in his white half-throne chair. As much as he wished he could resent what the Canadian was saying, there was no escaping the truth of the matter and the awareness of this showed on his face.

"Shortly before he died," Gagnon continued, "Cardinal Staffa asked to speak with me. He told me that in 1972, and again in 1975, in his capacity as Prefect of the Supreme Tribunal of the Apostolic Signatura he and Cardinal Oddi came to speak with Your Holiness about this very man *and* about Archbishop Annibale Bugnini. They supplied Your Holiness with evidentiary documentation to verify these extremely serious accusations. I include copies of the same in my report. They indicated that both men were and, I presume, still are, Freemasons with powerful Masonic connections — and that many of those connections, Holy Father, lead straight to the Institute for the Works of Religion [the Vatican Bank]."

"That is indeed true;" the Pope admitted, "Cardinals Staffa and Oddi came to us with the accusations, accusations that we turned over to Archbishop Benelli to investigate."

"And, may I ask what Archbishop Benelli's investigation found?" Gagnon inquired, already having been told the whole story by Giovanni Benelli himself, three years ago.

"Benelli concluded that the reports concerning Archbishop Bugnini were well-founded... On the basis of which we decided to send His Excellency to Iran as our nuncio. That was our Deputy's suggestion, and we agreed with it. That matter has been dealt with. We see no need to revisit it."

Édouard Gagnon removed his glasses and placed them on the desk. With his left hand he covered his eyes to hide the mounting frustration showing on his face. He put thumb and middle finger on his temples and pressed hard on them twice.

"Archbishop Bugnini, yes. But the accusations made against His Eminence, Cardinal Baggio, not so," the pope said.

"Not so?" Gagnon asked. He put his glasses back on and straightened up: "Again, Holy Father, with all due respect; is Your Holiness saying that the accusations against Cardinal Baggio were proved to be untrue, or were not true *enough?* I'm confused."

"At the time it was brought to our attention, we were

Archbishop Annibale Bugnini

assured by Secretary of State Villot that the accusations against Cardinal Baggio were unsubstantiated, and that the evidence presented was insufficient," the pope answered. "Soon thereafter, we spoke personally with Cardinal Baggio. We remember vividly that he denied the charges emphatically and *very* vociferously," the pope plainly and clearly recalled, "*very* vociferously," he repeated, "'Calumny,' he called them… It turned uglier still… His Eminence called for the dismissal of Archbishop Benelli… He *demanded* it. Of course, we would never entertain such a thing. Where would we be without Giovanni Benelli?" he asked. Again, he removed his glasses.

"Indeed, Holy Father; where would we be?"

The pope said nothing and Gagnon respected his silence by remaining as silent. Then, something very strange happened. Very slowly, Pope Paul put both hands on the two smaller tomes that Gagnon had placed before him and turned them around. When they were both facing Gagnon, the Pope put one atop the other, and then lifted both and set them upon the major report. He then pushed the set toward the seated Apostolic Visitor.

"Holy Father?" the baffled Visitor called for an explanation.

Pope Paul, however, remained completely silent. He turned his gaze away from the books and again sighed. The faintest look of delight came to his pale face — mostly likely, Gagnon assumed, caused by the bright ray of sunshine just breaking through the clouds and entering the tall library windows. It bathed the dark great room with welcome light.

Gagnon sat absolutely still. It was so quiet that, for the first time, he heard the desk clock marking the seconds. The old pope was thinking, and Gagnon would not interrupt.

When, after a long half a minute had passed, the pontiff straightened up again, reached for the glass of water, drank, and cleared his throat as if preparing to make an announcement.

"Dear brother," he began, his sad and tired eyes focused on Édouard Gagnon directly, "...You have before you a tired old man... who stands at the threshold of death and prepares himself, these days, to meet his Creator... and to answer for his many sins and faults..."

Archbishop Gagnon's eyes widened. Was he about to be asked to hear the pope's confession?! This was not in the script! Where was he going with this?

The pontiff took his eyes off the Visitor and began looking upward, not at the decorated ceiling, but somehow above and beyond it. He looked half lost, half blessed.

"Holy Father?" Gagnon called to him.

The pope looked again at his Apostolic Visitor. He put his hands on the three volumes of documents and pushed them even closer to their author, "We beg you to guard all of this, your invaluable research; keep it in your custody. Keep it safe and sound. Do not leave it here with us... Do *not* leave it here," he repeated, "When we cease to be the great burden we have become to this sacred office, you will please take this entire matter to our younger and stronger successor..."

"But, Your Holiness," Gagnon exclaimed, unwilling to believe his ears, "What are you saying?! These matters we're speaking about," he said and struck the three tomes three times with his knuckles, "and hundreds of others can't wait another day!" Exasperated, he continued: "A Freemason names our bishops! The Vatican Bank is on the verge of collapse! The rector of the Lateran University is laundering millions through it every year! And on and on and on. Your own Secretary of State, Holy Father, is your greatest adversary!"

Gagnon stopped talking long enough to control his

anger over these and a putrid world of other evils his investigation uncovered.

The pope said nothing.

"Holy Father, please tell me you're not serious," Gagnon recommenced, "All of this just cannot simply be ignored — and left for someone else to deal with — someone, somewhere, sometime in the distant future!"

"The proximate future, not the remote," the tired old man corrected, "We stand at the threshold of this world and the next. You'll not be made to wait long, Excellency," he declared this last part of his statement with the verve of an Old Testament prophet. Gagnon saw that he did not speak these words lightly - neither did they seem to weigh on him.

"We ask that you keep this invaluable information safe and to yourself… We charge you to explain everything you have right there, everything you tried to explain to us this morning — to our successor."

Édouard Gagnon simply could not believe his ears. Was this a nightmare? Some bizarre and horrible dream from which he could not awake? He himself had asked that no witnesses be present for this meeting and now, suddenly, he felt the urge to go after Villot and Casaroli and drag them back to tell him if this was real or not!

The bell from Saint Peter's campanile rang twice to mark ten-thirty. No, he wasn't dreaming. Yes, this was for real. And yes, the audience was about to end. But before it did, though his head was spinning, Édouard Gagnon had enough of his wits about him to make one final plea:

"If what Your Holiness says is *truly* what you want done," he soberly began, *"ainsi soit-il" [so be it.]* However…"

Gagnon noticed the pope struggling to push back his chair. As, more likely than not, he was about to attempt rising and standing on his own, Gagnon stood up at once and went to help him. Slowly the old man rose, and with a very pained expression on his pale face, stood, but bent over - with Archbishop Gagnon right next to him, just in case.

Eye to eye with the pontiff, Gagnon read between the lines and furrows on the old man's face: vulnerability, fatigue, pain, uncertainty, weakness.

"Holy Father," Gagnon said point blank, "I wish to ask a very special favor of you."

"Ask."

"Give me permission to share the contents of the Visitation with our most trusted mutual friend and confidant - with Cardinal Giovanni Benelli. Will you grant me that?"

Immediately the pontiff smiled.

"Willingly, dear brother, willingly. You have our permission to share these matters with Giovanni ... You very well may be saving yourself time and effort," he added.

"Holy Father?" the Canadian was confused.

A mischievous smile began to form on his lips, "Explaining the results of your Visitation to the Cardinal of Florence today might mean not having to explain them again to our successor," he smiled more broadly... "Yes, Excellency, Giovanni Benelli has our complete confidence. Most assuredly, you have our permission. Speak with him."

"And your blessing, Most Holy Father?" Gagnon entreated and kneeling, receive the benediction. With one hand on the desk to help himself up, he stood and saw that the pope was blessing the three volumes as well.

"Édouard Gagnon," the pontiff spoke his name and looked directly into the man's strong eyes.

"Holy Father?"

"For all your labors, for all we have put you through,

and all you've endured, Our Lord and Savior and His Blessed Mother thank you; the Church universal thanks you; and from the bottom of his heart, Peter [the pope himself] thanks you... *Éduardo Gagnon, venerabile fratello nostro: Arrivederci in Paradiso...*"

Archbishop Édouard Gagnon collected his materials.

"...*Adieu, Très Saint Père*," he answered the pope's final goodbye, then turned and left the his presence and the Apostolic Palace.

It was almost a quarter to eleven when a Swiss Guard's shrill whistle let me know that Archbishop Édouard Gagnon was at the elevator platform in the San Damaso Courtyard.

Knowing that he had gone into his meeting with three years' worth of material and only two hours in which to present it all, when he showed up now, with an hour and fifteen minutes to spare, I realized that something had gone very wrong.

I tossed the book I'd been reading onto the back seat, started the car and pulled up to the courtyard's four marble steps, exactly where I had dropped off the archbishop less than an hour ago.

Even from a distance of thirty feet I could see the serious look on my friend's usually cheerful visage. What's more, his book bag looked as full and heavy exiting the papal interview as when he entered it.

I ran around to open the passenger door.

"*Todo bien?*" [*Everything OK?*] I asked as he approached.

"I've had better mornings —and better outcomes," he answered dryly in Spanish and nothing more.

The archbishop's demeanor was strange: he wasn't exactly angry, but he was obviously perturbed, and deeply so.

The silence, as they say, was deafening, and I respected it for three full minutes —the time it took me to clear the gates at the Holy Office and get into the flow of Roman traffic.

"Did you want quiet all the way home?" I asked, to entice him to speak.

"Forgive me, Don Carlo, but a headache hit me - just as I got into the elevator," he said with his eyes closed.

"Should I stop at a pharmacy?"

"No," he answered, "the sooner we get home, the better."

As much as it killed me not to ask, "Were you able to speak to the pope about Mario Marini?" I did not. I knew much better. I'd never seen this good and always positive man in such a state.

That evening, the three of us, Archbishop Gagnon, Don Mario Marini and I, met in Gagnon's room. Our host looked quite a bit better than he had during his ride home from the Vatican. Right away, I understood why. About two hours ago, Archbishop Gagnon spoke by phone with the one and only person on earth who could set his spinning mind at ease: Cardinal Giovanni Benelli. They had agreed to meet in person, Friday evening, in some undisclosed place outside Rome - I assumed *Lago di Bracciano*. Nonetheless, Gagnon did not say where, nor did he ask me to drive him, nor did I offer to. The meeting would be completely private.

To ease Mario Marini's mind —though the news was not the positive report hoped for— Gagnon immediately told him that he had not had the opportunity to speak with the pope about his dismissal from the Secretariat of State by Jean Villot.

"You'll just have to believe me," Gagnon lamented, "it was neither the time nor the place. Regardless, it will be seen to," he assured Mario, "that I promise. Patience," he told him, "You have to learn what I'm having to relearn:" he said, "patience and forbearance."

Cortile San Damaso

Gagnon then prefaced what he was about to tell Mario and me about his audience with Pope Paul.

"While I am not now - nor, for that matter, will I ever be - at liberty to discuss specifics of the investigation itself," he then turned and looked me straight in the eyes: "nor is anyone who helped with any part of the investigation free to divulge things he may have seen or heard." Point made, he went on: "I *can* tell the two of you about this morning's audience."

Archbishop Gagnon recounted all he could about the audience, beginning with his "reverentially polite" reminder to the Supreme Pontiff that today's audience — like the first one, three years ago, when the pope and then-Deputy Benelli asked him to conduct the Apostolic Visitation of the Roman Curia— was to be private. It was meant for the pope and him alone. He then described the pope's "invitation" to Cardinal Villot and Archbishop Casaroli that they leave the study.

When the archbishop finished reporting the abruptly-terminated meeting, Mario Marini asked a few more questions on what he immediately called "the expulsion of the diplomat scoundrels."

I, on the other hand, was thoroughly intrigued with the pontiff's post-mortem instructions. "So, you're supposed to wait until he dies?! And then go and explain everything to the new pope!?" I asked incredulously. And, without looking before I leapt, added: "And what are you supposed to do if you die first?"

Many things I say are intentionally absurd, and they often caught Gagnon by surprise. He laughed when surprised, and I loved his laughter; it was innocent and executed with real glee.

Mario Marini began to reprimand me for my audacious lack of tact, when Édouard Gagnon began to chuckle: "My first thought, exactly!"

Then I asked seriously: "Is the pope ill? Is it something serious?"

"He's as healthy as a horse!" Mario chimed in.

"How old is he?" I asked.

"Eighty," answered Gagnon.

"Yes," Mario said, "But today's eighty isn't yesterday's eighty. The way he's cared for, Papa Montini could live to be a hundred!" And then Mario, a bit unsure of himself, asked Gagnon: "How did he look to you?"

"Not close to death? Right?" I asked.

"He's complex, our Holy Father, the pope," Gagnon answered after a little thought, "He's a man, I think, who would love to make everyone in the world happy - and keep everyone in the world happy - but he's learned how impossible that is. All I can tell you is that I've never known him to speak anything but the truth — regardless of the consequences," he mused, without explicit reference to *Humanae Vitae*, the pope's hugely controversial 1968 encyclical on Human Life.

"Then, you believe him when he says he's not long for this world?" I interrupted.

"That is what the good man told me, and I pass it along to you for what it's worth," he smiled. "Again, I say: I've never known him not to tell the truth."

The three of us spoke for over an hour before retiring. Mario Marini remained frustrated that Gagnon had not found an opportunity to discuss his plight with the pontiff. As for Gagnon, it did him good to have spoken with Benelli, and with Mario and me. We really had formed a society of friends, a priestly society of friends, and were proving to be very good for one another's morale.

That Friday evening, Archbishop Édouard Gagnon and Cardinal Giovanni Benelli met for an "extremely quiet" (not to say "clandestine") in-depth discussion at the *Chalet* on *Lago di Bracciano*. Archbishop Gagnon left our well-guarded residence with a full and heavy book bag and, unlike his frustrating visit with the Pope, returned later that night with the same book bag, now empty and very much lighter.

The next morning, Saturday morning, after Gagnon, Marini and I concelebrated Mass in the house chapel, we took our *caffé* and *cornetti* outside, in the far corner of the courtyard, so we could talk with no chance of being overheard, and as an extra precaution, we conversed in Spanish.

This time Gagnon arrived bearing good news — in particular, good news for Mario Marini.

"Benelli is on top of things," said Gagnon taking a healthy swallow of his *caffé-latte*, "…he's following your case closely and is helping you in ways you're unaware of."

"For example," Mario pushed the envelope.

"For example: a witness in your defense came forth from the Secretariat, a Villot underling who shall remain nameless. This good man is willing to testify that Villot waited, on purpose, for Benelli to leave the Vatican to dismiss you; that Villot wanted to make it impossible for you to be rescued by Benelli and, of course, through Benelli, the pope. The 'mystery-monsignor' heard this from Villot himself and swears to it. His sworn statement should be in the hands of your lawyer, Giuseppe Lobina, by the middle of next week. Cardinal Benelli insists you remain calm and patient; everything in your case is proceeding as it should and as it must. Like everything else in life: it's a question of time.

"Gio-van-ni Ben-el-li: Now there would be a pope!" said Mario Marini.

"Could that actually happen?" I wondered aloud.

"I believe that His Holiness's self-prophecy will come to pass sooner rather than later," said Archbishop Édouard Gagnon somberly, "… and as for papal elections," he shooed a bee away from his *cornetto*, "…in such matters, anything is possible."

"Sooner rather than later…" I repeated to myself.

THE POPE'S PROPHECY FULFILLED

August 6, 1978

Do not make the mistake of calling Tepatitlán a town. It is a *city* located about an hour west of Guadalajara. What's more, Tepatitlán is the capital of a region proudly known as *Los Altos [The Highlands]* of Jalisco. Should you ever be looking for the heart of Mexico, it is there you will find it beating strongly and nobly. That is certainly how it struck me when first I visited it in 1978. That summer, my archbishop, Francisco Javier Nuño y Guerrero, called me to Mexico for the months of July and August. He believed it would benefit me greatly to know the people and diocese for which I had been ordained. At the time, I was not pleased by my archbishop's decision - especially since he had agreed to "donate" me to the service of the Holy See, which meant I would not be living or working in Mexico. In retrospect, it was one of the best things that ever happened to me, and it would have been ludicrous for the good archbishop to have acted otherwise.

In the early evening of August sixth, the Feast of the Transfiguration, dear Sister Petra phoned from the retreat house where I was rooming to the nearby *Sagrada Familia* Parish where I was helping out. Immediately, and in a very sad tone of voice, she asked if I had heard the news.

"...Oh, *Padre Carlos!* The Holy Father —he has died, *Padre,*" she announced in that soft, sad and somber voice usually reserved for the loss of family members.

Like everyone else, I knew that the pope had been in very poor health recently, nonetheless, the news of his death took me by surprise, and my throat seemed to close for a panicky moment. But there was more.

"And, *Padre*; a Monsignor just phoned. From Italy."

"From Rome?" I asked, hoping to narrow it down.

"No, *Padre*; he said he was calling from ... *Rwanda??*" sister pronounced uncertainly.

"Ravenna?" I made a wild guess.

"Yes," she answered, "That's what he said: *Ravenna!* He wants that you return his call — he said, "at once," *Padre*," she said and preceded to read me the phone number the "Rwandan" gave her, "... He said to call *immediately* because it's already late at night there."

For two days straight I tried to contact Mario in Ravenna. But, in central Mexico the *"tiempo de lluvias"* [rainy season] had not yet ended, and Tepatitlán and surrounding areas had just endured a torrential rain, thunder and lightning storm the likes of which would not soon be forgotten, and in the wake of which great sectors of Los Altos had been left without electricity and telephone service.

I tried again, on the third day after he had called me, to phone him back. By my calculations it was eight or nine at night where he was. In a back office of the *Sagrada Familia*, I sat down on the wobbly metal chair at the wobbly metal desk. The incessant humming of the fluorescent ceiling lights filled the long periods of silence as I waited and waited. Finally, after five decades of the rosary, I made contact with an international operator who, after another fifteen minutes -- the Sorrowful Mysteries, this time -- was able to get an international line.

For obvious reasons, my Dad's nickname for *Teléfonos de México* came to mind and, while listening carefully for the long waited ring, I quietly repeated it: "Taco Bell."

Although only two months had passed since Marini, Gagnon and I were together, it seemed longer than a year. I didn't just miss the two of them; I missed the three of us.

I missed after-Mass breakfasts with Archbishop Capucci. I missed classes at the Gregorian and philosophy discussions with Professors Navone and Becker. I missed the drives up *Via Trionfale* and the visits with Madre Pascalina. I missed the banter and joking with Naldo and Silvio in between work at the Information Office. Stuck in the middle of Mexico — and at a time like this! — made me Rome-sick and left me frustrated.

Even now, days after learning that Pope Paul had died, I felt like doing something I had not done in years: find a room I could lock myself in alone, sit down in a corner, and cry. Of course, I wouldn't actually do such a thing. A tear shed now would be one shed out of self-pity, and nothing is more unmanly than a man completely self-absorbed.

"Charlie?" Mario answered on the second ring.

It was so good to hear his booming voice again. So good!

Mario gave me a quick rundown on his situation.

As everyone who can does, in August he escaped the brutal heat of Rome, and made a hasty retreat home, to pleasantly cooler Ravenna and the spectacular Adriatic. It had been his first summer without a vacation since he was a boy in post WWII years. For two weeks every summer, he and his lifelong friend Padre Andres Baeza would meet in Texas or Arizona or Colorado and explore some different part of the American Southwest. This summer, however, Benelli encouraged him to stay close to Rome - and what Benelli said, Marini did. With the pope's death, it seemed, once again, that Benelli knew what he was talking about.

"I leave tomorrow for Rome — if you can believe that," Mario reported and huffed.

"Why?" I asked.

"You did hear that the pope died, no?" he asked with pointed sarcasm.

"The pope died!? Good God, Mario! When!?" I exclaimed even more sarcastically.

"Humph," he grunted, "The funeral is Saturday, and then begin the preparations for the conclave! Why am I going back to Rome?" he huffed again at the banality of my question, "Because *El Mariscal*" wants me there, that's why."

When left with no other communications option but the telephone —a contrivance he never fully trusted— Mario spoke —or tried to speak— in code. He'd slip up occasionally, but discretion was the idea. For example: the Pope was usually *El Patrón [The Boss]*; Giovanni Benelli was always *El Mariscal [The Marshall]*; Édouard Gagnon was *El Colombiano [The Colombian]*; Monsignore Guglielmo Zannoni was *Il Polento [po'lento - a little slow]*; his lawyer, Monsignor Giuseppe Lobina was *"El Lobo" [The Wolf]*, and when it wasn't just "Charlie," I was *El Gringo* or *Gringito*. Not surprisingly, he christened his nemesis, the Frenchman Cardinal Villot, *"René-Rana" [René the Frog, the Spanish name for Kermit the Frog]*.

Any new personality who might enter into the conversation was renamed by Mario on the spot. Often enough, I was left to figure out the identity of this one or that one, solely on a contextual basis - at times challenging; usually funny; always interesting.

"Doesn't he know you don't attend state functions?" I toyed with him just a little.

"Nor will I attend this one," he answered abruptly, "I've said my prayers for the repose of the good man's soul, and will continue to say Masses for him. I owe him more than I could ever pay back... He paid my way through seminary when my own parents rejected me; he saw to my doctoral studies at the Gregorian University and my residence at the *Collegio Lombardo*; he entrusted me with a coveted position and gave me an office across the hall from his own... But, as much as I owe him, I'm not going anywhere near that place [the Vatican] until my case is resolved."

"I understand," I answered honestly, "But '*El Mariscal*' wants you in Rome, now? Why?"

"Don't be naïve! What do you think he wants to talk about, gardening!? Horse racing?! He wants to talk to me *and 'El Colombiano,'* about upcoming events, of course! It took a day and a half of phone calls to locate '*El Colombiano!*' He's back home in Montreal, visiting family!" he said, as if there were something wrong with that.

"You mean, like you are right now?" I could not help but interject.

"I'm not on the other side of the world; I don't need days to rearrange my travel plans and plane reservations! I board a train, and in five or six hours I'm back in Rome."

Mario was seriously apprehensive about the upcoming papal election — seriously apprehensive, which explained some of his brusqueness whenever the subject was broached. I had watched his apprehension increase this past year — even before his dismissal.

The "next conclave" evoked in him a dread similar to Cardinal Dino Staffa's own. Mario and Staffa had been close friends for years. Last year, shortly before his death, Staffa spoke long and hard with Mario Marini. He then spoke with Édouard Gagnon, in his capacity as Apostolic Visitor to the Curia, to share his severe trepidation. "My recurring nightmare," he said to both men, on separate occasions, "is having to pledge obedience to the new pontiff, and having to kiss the Fisherman's Ring on the hand of the first Freemason Pope!"

Mario described Staffa to me as literally trembling when he pronounced those words. And Cardinal Dino Staffa was no slouch!

"Pray," Mario almost shouted, "like you've never prayed before; pray that '*El Mariscal*' reaches the number needed!" In typical Marini fashion, he added: "And be specific when you address heaven. I've always taught you the importance of succinctness and specificity in prayer," he stated and by continuing to talk, robbed me of the chance to say that this was the very first time I had heard him make such a pronouncement. "Seventy-five! That's the exact number Benelli needs!" he said, having broken his own rule about not mentioning "El Mariscal's" name in public or by phone, "Seventy-five!" he repeated.

"But his age, Mario," I interpolated, "He's awfully young," I foolishly brought up Benelli's mere fifty-seven years on planet earth, "and 'El Colombiano' says 'El Mariscal' is too much a realist not to know this."

"You're really a defeatist, you know that? 'Young' is exactly what we need!" he shouted so that I moved the receiver at a safer distance from my ear, "Catholic, young, a proper and substantial pair of balls," he enunciated each word clearly "and saint enough to stop 'Lucifer-incarnate' dead in his tracks!"

He didn't actually mention "Sebastiano Baggio." He didn't have to; the satanic reference sufficed.

"And, for your information, Gringito, Mastai-Ferretti was only fifty-four!" Mario averred, trumping my "Benelli's awfully young" card with a "Pio Nono [Pope Pius IX] was-even-three-years-younger" trick of his own.

"But what if…" I began to ask but immediately regretted it - not just for what Benelli's loss would mean for the Church, but for what it would mean for Mario Marini, whose ongoing case against "René" kept him suspended in a virtual limbo.

To my surprise, Marini answered my unfinished question coolly: "No wartime general worth his salt goes into battle without an alternate plan of attack." He laughed quietly, "Our general [Benelli] has two."

"Two? Who?!" I asked excitedly —as if Mario Marini

would pronounce their names in a phone call! And via international cable, to boot!

"Remember Saint Malachy?" he asked.

He referred to the eleventh-century Irish saint who wrote an apocryphal description of all the popes, from his day until the last day.

"I thought you didn't believe in those things," I rebuffed.

"Old wives' tales!" he mockingly affirmed what I thought, "But that's not the point. You asked a question; I'll give you an answer."

"OK."

"Find the title your Irish saint gives the next pope, then *'cut the moon in half.'*"

"What? What in the blazes are you talking about?"

He laughed and continued the teasing: "Listen: cut 'moon' in half;" he said it this time without the definite article, "and you'll have an easy clue to the man's identity. You're smart," he snickered, "you told me once, you'd make a good detective. Well, I just gave you the key clue, 'Columbo!'" He taunted me with (of all people) Peter Falk! ("Columbo" was the only RAI-TV program Mario ever watched — and only then on rare occasions.) "The alternative to that is a foreigner. Not likely," he dismissed it as too absurd. "No, if it isn't himself, it will be his friend, the half-moon."

"If *'El Mariscal'* does win, that would be the end of your case against *'René'*."

"Ha!" he grunted a low laugh, "You mean, it would be the end of *'René'* altogether! He would send that arrogant Frenchman packing before the white smoke cleared the sky!"

"One way or another, he'll win," I said to encourage my slightly anxious friend, "Let's pray that God's will be done!"

"And may God's will be our will!" Marini's bass voice boomed the rather ambiguous theological finale across the transatlantic cables.

Then came the all-too- familiar click indicating that the conversation had ended. Mario Marini was never one for long goodbyes — in fact, he had no time for "goodbyes," of any real length.

"Sleep well, *mi querido capitán!*" I bade him good night.

After early Mass the following morning, I walked downtown, to the *portales,* and stopped at *La Farmacia Relampago.* The pharmacist saw me buying a copy of *El Excelsior.* He introduced himself, Alfonso Martin del Campo, and invited me to his back office where I could have "a serious place to read and a serious cup of coffee to help stomach the news." I willingly accepted and he showed me to his desk.

There it was, on page three; a complete list of the eligible cardinal electors. And there he was: **BENELLI, Giovanni; Age 57; Archbishop of Florence.**

But, only when I saw it in print did Mario's teasing "key clue" click: **LUCIANI, Albino; Age 66; Patriarch of Venice.** I said it out loud: "LU-ciani; *mezza luna [half the moon]: LU-na)!* I smiled more broadly when I learned that LUciani, former President of the Italian Episcopal Conference, was born in Bel*lu*no. That cinched it.

I left the pharmacy determined to spend all my extra time from that moment until I heard *"Habemus Papam!"* storming heaven in prayer.

At least that *was* my intention, until later that afternoon when —ironically, during prayer and meditation— I received another significant phone call. This one was from my archbishop, Don Francisco Javier Nuño y Guererro ordering me to report, as soon as possible, to the cathedral in nearby San Juan de los Lagos, where more than one million pilgrims, from as far away as Mexico City, were about to descend and pay filial respects to the Virgin of San Juan on her feast day, August 15, the Solemnity of the Assumption. "And," the soft-spoken archbishop declared: "with a handful of marvelous exceptions, all one million of them are in serious need of confession."

For seven oppressively hot days, from the ninth to the fifteenth of August, 1978, mine was the wooden middle seat in an old and worn confessional for twelve to sixteen hours a day, while the parade of unwashed humanity, most of whom had been walking for weeks, entered the cathedral confines by the hundreds of thousands bent on getting a closer view of the diminutive Blessed Virgin Mary.

When that physically, emotionally, and spiritually draining week came to a blessed end I returned to Tepatitlán, went immediately to my room in the retreat house, and collapsed on my bed and remained there for fourteen uninterrupted hours before resuming work at the *Sagrada Familia* Parish.

I woke up the next morning knowing that the final countdown had begun and that soon Gagnon, Marini, and Zannoni would meet together. They certainly would be keeping close tabs on all things Vatican — especially my friend, Mario Marini. Had Benelli already spoken with Gagnon, I wondered? Had he spoken with Mario? If "the will of God" was not ours, what kind of a man was "Half-Moon" Albino Luciani? That name... It had a sort of Mafioso ring to it. I smiled at myself imagining the Cardinal Patriarch of Venice being related to Lucky Luciano!

On the *Farmacia Relampago* wall calendar I had thumbtacked next to the empty bookcase in my small office, I began to "X" off the days; ten more until the voting commenced in the Sistine Chapel, beneath the terrible, penetrating, and all-knowing gaze of Michelangelo's *Christ of the Last Judgement*.

THE SMILING POPE
August 26, 1978

As much as I wanted to be in Saint Peter's Square for the September 3rd coronation of the new pope, changing my *Pan Am* flight proved impossible. Correction: most likely a sign of things to come, the new pontiff had changed the "coronation" to the much less monarchical and much more democratic-sounding "inauguration." Either way, I missed it.

Likewise, the new pontiff made a name for himself by combining the names of his two immediate predecessors, John XXIII and Paul VI. Soon after his historic election in the Sistine Chapel, from the Loggia of the Blessings Cardinal Pericles Felici introduced him to the world (and the world to him) as *"Ioannes Paulus"*.

After my "Mexican summer," and before returning to Rome, I went home to visit family and friends for a week. So, rather than standing in Saint Peter's Square and witnessing the papal "inauguration" in person, I was sitting in our Saint Paul, Minnesota living room and following the event via satellite — which, thanks to central air conditioning, all the "comforts of home," and the miracle of television and cameras with close-focus lenses, afforded me a spectacular view of everything and saved me from a two-hour roasting under the merciless Roman sun.

And, yes, it goes without saying that the new pope was the very man Mario Marini (so invaluably assisted by Saint Malachy!) cryptically informed me it would be during our transatlantic conversation.

I didn't usually take a taxi into Rome, but after a

three-hour delay at JFK, an awful flight, and the hour-and-a-half "spaghetti rigamarole" of clearing passport and customs at Leonardo Da Vinci Airport, I was too exhausted to deal with luggage and a standing-room-only bus ride into *Stazione Termini.*

The taxi pulled up to the front gate of the Lebanese Residence. I paid the cabbie and walked to the trunk for my luggage, from where I saw, parked directly across the street, the brown Mercedes from the Syrian Embassy. I gave an informal salute to the familiar man behind the wheel. His young "co-pilot," evidently an apprentice-spy, stared at me coldly, but Mohammed smiled and gave me a thumbs-up, no-need-to-frisk, welcome home. This was the first time since Archbishop Hilarion Capucci had arrived that I did not see the Israelis' van. Still, the modern brick building was in one piece, standing firmly, which meant that Capucci was at home and safe and sound.

It was just before noon when I opened the front door to *Fratelli Bandiera* number 19. Immediately I was hit with the sensational aromas of too much garlic, too much onion, mint, and roasting lamb — all of it without the faintest hint of simmering tomato sauce that could easily trick the famished traveler into thinking that something Italian awaited him. But, no! Sor Olga knew I was arriving today and had prepared my Middle Eastern favorites: *laham mishwe* with freshly crushed *toum* and chopped *tabbouleh.* God love her!

Leaving my largest suitcase in the porter's office, I practically ran to the staircase and took the marble steps two at a time. It was Saturday and I knew Mario would be home. Between the second and third floors I called out in Romanesco: *"A Do' Mar-i-eu!"* [Hey, Don Mario!]

The second from the last door of the corridor flew open: "Charlie! Charlie Murr!" came the deep bass welcome. As we gave each other a long and hard Mexican *abrazo,* the door next to Mario's opened: *"Bienvenido, Don Carlo!"*

Archbishop Édouard Gagnon exclaimed with the broadest, warmest smile, "This house has been too quiet without you!" he joked, "We missed you," he said.

No sooner had Gagnon and I embraced when the last door on the third floor opened, the one at the end of the corridor, and Archbishop Hilarion Capucci joined the impromptu welcome ceremony: *"Père Charlot!"*[1] he exclaimed and gave me three cheek kisses, then turned to acknowledge Gagnon and Marini with a smile and a nod, *"Bienvenue,"* he welcomed, *"Et ton voyage, s'est bien passé? [And your trip, it went smoothly?"]*

"Ça s'est très bien passé, Excellence," [It went very well, Your Excellency.]

"How good to have you with us again," he continued, "Such a mundane affair, breakfast, since you left," he grinned, shook his head and rolled his eyes, "We'll talk later," he said, excused himself and took his leave to enter the elevator.

The three of us, Gagnon, Marini and I, decided that 1) I needed to have a bite to eat and — since I told them that I hadn't slept in 30 hours— 2) take a serious nap, and 3) meet in Gagnon's room for an *aguardiente* before 4) leaving at 7:30 for *mandorle* and pizza at *Birreria Marconi.*

"I'll call *'Er Dottore,'*" Mario said, referring to the eldest waiter at *Marconi's* by his Roman nickname, *"er dottore* [the doctor, or "Doc"] "and have him reserve the back corner table for us, so we can talk." He then asked Archbishop Gagnon, "Does 7:30 work for you, *Monsignore?"*

"That would be just fine," the Canadian answered.

"A lot has happened here in your absence," Mario told me.

Édouard Gagnon's eyebrows rose at least three centimeters higher than the frame of his glasses as, with a

---

1 *"Charlot"* was the name of Charlie Chaplin's character "The Tramp." Archbishop Capucci called me this because I made him laugh.

head nod, he said without saying it that, indeed, *very much* had happened in my absence.

It took me a moment to remember where I was but when I did, I sat up and forthrightly addressed the alarm clock situation. It was 5:30, which meant I had just enough time to unpack my bags, take a shower, and recite vespers before conferring with my two senior confreres at 6:30.

The archbishop did the honors, and handed Mario and me each a small terracotta cup, slightly larger than a shot glass.

"Eduardo and Eulalia Martinez —a wonderful Colombian couple from Medellin, a beautiful family— send me a bottle of *aguardiente* every year at Christmas," he prefaced and then raised his cup and respectfully offered: "To His Holiness, the Pope; *Vivat in aeternum [long life]*."

Mario and I raised our cups slightly and answered in kind: "*In aeternum vivat*," and then took a cautious sip of the strong potion. Gagnon offered this Colombian fire-water only on special occasions. I bit my tongue to keep from blurting out what I always thought when I drank this "treat": "I've never actually tasted paint remover, but I imagine it tastes something like this!"

"And Cardinal Benelli?" I asked to get the ball rolling.

"Fine," said Gagnon, "doing very well. We met and spoke before the conclave - and once afterwards," he added demurely.

"The king-maker," Mario proudly interjected.

"Undoubtedly," I agreed.

"He entered the conclave knowing his friends from his enemies," Mario continued, "and he knew exactly how many he had of both, and who they were." He smirked, "There's no greater realist on earth than the Deputy. He knew he didn't have the votes —not the seventy-five needed. But he also knew that he had more than any other candidate. He knew he was in control. As Monsignor

Archbishop Hilarion Capucci

Gagnon says, he knew that long before they intoned the *Veni, Creator Spiritus.*

Édouard Gagnon chuckled and agreed: "Realistic, self-controlled, pragmatic. The hardest-working man I know."

"Quite a compliment coming from you, Excellency, since you're the hardest working man *I* know," I said honestly, and, making a playful bow to Mario, added, "Present company excepted."

"Humph," he sluffed off the pretended slight, "Benelli would have been perfect, but, Albino Luciani, Benelli's own candidate, will be just fine with Benelli by his side."

"How's that?" I asked.

"Our new pontiff has asked the Cardinal of Florence to be his new Secretary of State," Mario proudly announced, "Has he not, *Monseigneur*?"

"He has," Gagnon confirmed.

"Wow!" I exclaimed. "I thought —I mean, I read somewhere that the pope confirmed everyone in the Curia; that they were to remain right where they were; no changes would be made."

"You see, *Padre Carlos*," Gagnon explained with paternal gentleness, "when a new pope takes office, the Prefects from the previous pontificate present their written resignations. That's just how it's done. Everywhere. In fact, with every outgoing and incoming administration. And rightly so," he said, accentuating the obvious sense of the practice with a slight shrug of the shoulders.

"But you're saying that Pope John Paul *didn't* do that."

"It's not the end of the world," Marini declared, "The mistake of a *novillero [apprentice matador]*, that's all. He shouldn't actually have instructed those scoundrels not to resign, but he did. So?" he smirked, "They're in place *pro tempore* - until further notice," he said more emphatically, "It only shows how unprepared Luciani was. He hadn't even entertained the possibility of leaving the conclave as pope. Why, he himself voted for Benelli!"

"How could you possibly know that?" I asked, aware of the solemn oath of silence each cardinal took regarding the election process.

"Albino Luciani might be shy, but one thing he didn't hide was his support for Benelli. Prior to entering the

Sistine Chapel, he told quite a few folks that the best pope for our times is Cardinal Benelli… It's public knowledge."

"They've been close friends for years," Gagnon concurred, "Benelli helped him greatly during his tenure as President of the Italian Episcopal Conference."

"Even so," Mario was still chewing on the confirmation issue, "It wasn't prudent to reconfirm all the curial department heads. Imagine how pleased it must have made Villot and Baggio."

"When did he ask him?" I asked the archbishop.

"Sorry? When did who ask what?"

"The Holy Father," I clarified, "when did he ask Cardinal Benelli to be his Secretary of State?"

Édouard Gagnon remained pensive and silent again.

It suddenly occurred to me how much Mario had come to view everything concerning what was best for the entire Catholic Church through the lens of the drama of his dismissal from the Secretariat of State and his ongoing fight for reinstatement.

"Last Thursday," Gagnon gave voice to something he obviously had been pondering, "the Holy Father had a lengthy private audience with Cardinal Benelli. Benelli called me immediately afterwards and asked to see me. It was urgent, he said. I met with him and he told me straight out, no beating around the bush." Then, looking at Mario, "You know how he is when it comes to important business."

"Humph," Marini snorted, "I certainly do."

"Well," he continued, "His Holiness is asking for the results of the Apostolic Visitation. He wants me to present them and explain some of the finer points of interest. Naturally, I agreed! It's what I had tried to present to Pope Paul, God rest him."

"*Ma, questo é stupendo!*" Mario exclaimed in Italian — then, almost immediately, he looked somewhat annoyed.

Was his vexation caused by the fact that Giovanni Benelli hadn't thought to share this stupendous news with him? In any event, with Villot gone and Benelli in his place, Marini's reinstatement was as good as done.

"Can I count on you to drive me?" Archbishop Gagnon asked me directly.

"To your audience with the pope? You know you can!" I responded enthusiastically, "Give me a little advance notice, and I'll have the car polished to such a high gloss that the guards in San Damaso will have to look away as we approach!"

"Did Benelli say when your meeting would be?" Mario inquired

"'Soon,' is what he told me," Gagnon responded, "That's all I know at the moment."

The strong-willed Canadian tried to conceal his great satisfaction with these new developments, but he simply could not.

"Shouldn't we get to Marconi's before *'er dottore'* gives our table away to more deserving patrons?"

"Let's go!" Mario and I both said at the same time.

"OK. No argument," Édouard Gagnon announced as he rose from his chair, "When the bill arrives, it's mine. Tonight, gentlemen, dinner's on me," he said, and concluded with a self-deprecating laugh, "How easy it is to play the openhanded millionaire when it comes to six beers and three pizzas! I'm just grateful, Don Mario, that you didn't make reservations at Charlie's!"

This friendly jab did not refer to me, but to *"Charly's Sauciere,"* a great little hole-in-the-wall restaurant near the Colosseum, run by Charly, an eccentric Swiss friend of ours — but one with a rather pricey menu.

On Monday, the eighteenth of September, I registered at the Gregorian for four graduate courses in philosophical anthropology and an intriguing weekly seminar on Miguel de Unamuno. From there I made my way across the city, arriving at my work at the Vatican Information Office fifteen minutes late. Having not seen my co-workers for months, we spent some time kissing, hugging, joking, laughing, and catching up. Even as we got down to work, there was convivial, back and forth talk. Naturally, much was said about Pope Paul VI's death, and more was said about the new man, this "smiling pope", John Paul.

Like millions of others, I couldn't wait to see the man in person, to get a real sense of him. In a world that seemed to have lost its way, many of us looked to this particular man, this Successor of Saint Peter and Vicar of Jesus Christ on Earth, for guidance and hope.

That following Wednesday morning, at ten minutes to eleven, I asked permission from our director, General Santicchioli, to absent myself from the office for fifteen minutes, time enough to walk over to the *Aula Nervi* and get a glimpse of the new Pope during his general audience. Permission granted, I took the shortcut through the back doors of the Information Office and stood near the Swiss Guards at the Nervi vestibule. Police whistles blew as gendarmes waved the black Mercedes around the corner of the Teutonic College chapel.

No sooner had the car come to a halt when, as if out of nowhere, two men in black suits appeared and opened the car's back doors. Out stepped the pope. For a fleeting moment, our eyes met and he smiled and waved as he passed by. Yes, as people were saying, there was something extraordinarily genuine in that timid smile. Remarkable. Yet, how strange to see another man taking the place of the only man I'd ever seen be pope: Paul VI. Until then, I had only heard the word "countersensational" used in certain philosophy courses. This was the first time I experienced it.

I watched closely as Albino Luciani took an unsure step up to the *sedia gestatoria* platform and seated himself. He held tight to its two arms as, in regimented fashion,

Pope John Paul I

twelve tuxedo-clad *sediari pontifici [pontifical chair porters]*, six on one side, six on the other, took hold of the two side poles and in one swift, synchronized move lifted the pontiff above their heads and rested the poles on their shoulders. The curtains parted, the thousands who had been waiting, broke into thunderous cheering and applause, and the papal entourage left the vestibule, moving through the hall to the front stage.

Turning to make my way back to the office, I enjoyed a feeling of tremendous satisfaction. Somehow, just by seeing him, by catching the look in his eyes for that fraction of a second, I knew that Albino Luciani had the makings of an outstanding Pope. Knowing from Archbishop Gagnon that the new pope had already asked Cardinal Giovanni Benelli to be his right-hand man, his Secretary of State, I was certain that this new pontificate was off to a great start. Together, these two men would give the Church the leadership and direction she so desperately needed right then! Luciani and Benelli might have what it would take to make as magnificent a team as Saint Pope Pius X and his Secretary of State, Blessed Rafael Merry-del Val.

What was to prevent it?!

THE SECOND DELIVERY ATTEMPT

September 25, 1978

"Are you nervous?" I asked my episcopal passenger.

"'Anxious' might be a better word," Édouard Gagnon said quietly, "I've been anticipating this day since that other one," he turned and looked me in the eyes, "the last time you drove me to a papal audience." He smiled, "I still haven't gotten over that surprise. To have the pope tell you that he's no longer in condition to deal with the results of your investigation…"

"His investigation, the investigation he commissioned," I interjected.

"The last time I spoke with him… the last time I saw him alive…" he stopped in mid-sentence, "…There was always something prophetic about Pope Paul," he mused, "A profoundly spiritual man, to be sure."

Traffic slowed to a standstill. Rather than wait for things to clear up, I told the archbishop not to worry, but to hold on. Making a hard left, I did a couple of quick back-and-forths into the opposite lane (carefully avoiding a cliff), and took off in the opposite direction.

"And you've never had an accident in all your years driving here, eh?" he asked in wonderment —not to be funny.

To put my friend at ease, I chatted on, assuring him that everything he was about to discuss with the pope would be well-received. "I'm sure that Cardinal Benelli has spoken at length with His Holiness and has explained in detail that the result of your investigation into the Roman Curia offers a blueprint for purging and rebuilding his central government."

"Yes, Cardinal Benelli assured me of the same... However, he will not accept the position of Secretary of State until Baggio is removed from the Congregation for Bishops."

Of course, there were many things I didn't understand about the workings of the Church, but there were many I understood perfectly well.

"And Cardinal Villot? Who tells him it's time to go?"

Édouard Gagnon thought about that a moment. As far as I could see, he was not searching for an answer to my question —he knew the answer— but rather, he was asking himself whether he should be speaking with me about such things. At any rate, finally he did answer me: "It seems Cardinal Villot has already seen to that himself. He submitted his resignation the day after the election. The pope accepted it but asked that he remain until such time as his replacement could be found. The cardinal suggested Archbishop Casaroli."

"Casaroli?" I scoffed, "Villot, Junior."

"The pope had already decided on Cardinal Benelli."

"Then, why doesn't Cardinal Benelli deal with Baggio when he takes the reins? As Secretary of State, he'd have the power to banish the Freemason to Cucamonga if he wanted to."

"I'm not sure where Cucamonga is, exactly," Gagnon (a fellow W.C. Fields fan) said with a smile, "But what about the Cucamongese?" he paused in doubt for a moment.

"Somewhere in California," I responded. "And I believe the inhabitants prefer 'Cucamongolians,' to Cucamongese," I suggested with a deadpan expression and managed to get another rise out of Gagnon.

"Well," he chuckled again, "whatever they call

themselves, I'm sure they have community standards. What possible sin could they have committed to deserve the Prefect of the Sacred Congregation for Bishops as a penance?!" he asked the rhetorical question in jest, but shook his head in real wonderment over the entire scandalous Baggio matter.

"Right," I agreed, "but Cardinal Benelli could see to Baggio himself, couldn't he? From what little I've observed of our new pontiff, he is both intelligent and devout, but he does not give the impression of being very strong. Strong-willed," I qualified.

"Maybe that's just the point," Gagnon added knowingly, "Maybe Cardinal Benelli insists he do this first major change in his pontificate himself. You know," he said, then thought a moment for the American maxim to come to him, "take the bull by the horns."

We entered the gates to Vatican City and sped around the back of Saint Peter's Basilica. I slowed down considerably, to a dignified speed, just before entering the Cortile San Damaso, and drove up as close as I could get to the stairs to the elevator.

The dry-run, four months ago, with Paul VI, made today's exercise seem like child's play. It was, in the memorable words attributed (like so many) to Yogi Berra: "It's Déjà vu all over again!"

I got out of the Fiat, as did Archbishop Édouard Gagnon. He put the violet zucchetto on his head, readjusted his cassock sash and pectoral cross, and reached back into the car for his black leather bookbag containing the collection of documents powerful enough to sink a battleship. Then the archbishop surprised me again, asking for my blessing. Humbly, with embarrassment a sinful man and imperfect priest imparted his blessing to a saint and scholar, a noble man bent on reforming Christ's Church on earth.

"It will go well for you, Excellency," I said, "It will go better than you ever imagined!"

Archbishop Édouard Joseph Gagnon smiled, and with steady resolve in his soul, was on his way.

When Archbishop Édouard Gagnon exited the elevator, he was met by a very subdued Cardinal Jean Villot. They walked down the corridor side by side but, unlike four months ago, this morning's conversation was minimal. When they reached the papal apartment the two Swiss Guards at either side of the doors, stiffened to attention and gave a crisp heel-click salute. Villot opened and held the door for Gagnon and then followed slightly behind him. "Archbishop Gagnon," the new Pope called out from the other side of the long room, "Good morning, Your Excellency," he said and stood to greet his guest.

The famous smile, now aimed directly and solely at him, made Gagnon profoundly aware that he was in the presence of Christ's Vicar. Though false pride was nowhere to be found in Édouard Joseph Gagnon, he felt deeply humbled by the sincerity and warmth of the man who owned that welcoming smile. He walked up to him and kissed the fisherman's ring, and the fisherman invited him to be seated in the chair directly facing him.

Cardinal Jean Villot asked the Pope if there was anything else he might need. Pope John Paul answered politely that there was not, and Jean Villot dutifully disappeared.

Albino Luciani and Gagnon did not know each other very well, but they had met several times. Fortifying their mutual respect was their great admiration for Giovanni Benelli, who, not surprisingly, had already spoken highly and at great length of each man to the other. In fact, Papa Luciani and Gagnon somehow felt they had known each other for years. Such are the first sparks of friendship.

Before getting down to business, Pope John Paul let Archbishop Gagnon know that he fully shared Paul VI's apprehensions; that "the smoke of Satan" most certainly had entered the Church and now, to a very real degree, was asphyxiating her; that many of the hierarchy, priests, and religious were undergoing a crisis of faith.

Pope John Paul expressed his deep gratitude to the Apostolic Visitor for the three years of dedication and painstaking labors he put into the delicate investigation.

"Is what we hear true?" Pope John Paul inquired, "That vandals broke into your rooms and offices because of this investigation? That you received death threats?"

"It is true, Your Holiness."

"Why did you not request accommodations inside Vatican City?"

"Holy Father?" Gagnon asked for clarification.

"For security. For your personal protection."

Now understanding the question, Édouard Gagnon could not keep himself from laughing.

"Holy Father!" he chuckled, "Saltare dalla padella nella brace [From the frying pan into the fire]?!" he asked, "With all respect, Holy Father," Gagnon could not completely wipe the grin off his face, "Those ruffians — the ones who ransack rooms and threaten lives;" he looked squarely at the Pope, "where do you think they live?!"

John Paul's innocent face simultaneously registered disbelief and belief.

"Madonna Santa!" he exclaimed.

"No, no," Gagnon shook his head, "I'm fine right where I am, Holy Father. I live two doors down from an accused Palestinian terrorist, and I feel much safer there than I believe Your Holiness feels here."

The pontiff's whole demeanor changed noticeably. Hardly a trace of the smile was detectable and his attention to the Apostolic Visitor's remarks and observations was more concentrated. He undid three buttons on his cassock and pulled from his vest pocket two folded sheets of paper with handwritten notes on them. He then moved several blank sheets of paper closer to himself and cleared his voice.

"As Your Excellency can imagine, there are a number of subjects about which we have been advised to give you close hearing," he began, obviously following Giovanni Benelli's instructions to the letter, "Three of these matters we would like to address at once."

"Of course, Holy Father."

"First of all, very serious accusations have been made against a number of Curia members. I myself," he said, forgetting the majestic plural, "have seen a list of names and have been hearing these claims for two or three years now," he said, "My straightforward questions to you are: Is there any truth to these allegations? If so, do you know who and how many they are? And, again, if such is the case," the pope added cautiously, "can you substantiate these claims with verifiable proof?" he asked, and slowly reached for one of the two ballpoint pens at his disposal.

Gagnon lifted his black leather book bag, placed it on the desktop, opened it and took out three tomes. Briefly, he explained each one: the thickest contained a chronological history of his investigation, with significant results obtained from hundreds of person-to-person interviews, department by department. A thinner tome held pertinent documentation. The thinnest tome contained his conclusion and suggested steps to be taken to remedy "the most serious problems" that — as Gagnon himself clarified pointedly for the new Pontiff— "avevo scoperto o, con il permesso di Sua Santità, 'dissotterrato'" [I discovered or, with Your Holiness's permission, 'unearthed'"].

The archbishop opened the middle volume at one of the several protruding tabs, and turned the tome to face the pope.

John Paul's eyes moved as he scanned the two pages, otherwise he remained motionless and silent. Gagnon wondered: Did he know his mouth was wide open?

"Document forty-one:" Archbishop Gagnon interrupted the pontiff's mute stillness and placed his index finger on the top of the page, "His Eminence, Cardinal Sebastiano Baggio; Document forty-two: His Excellency, Bishop Annibale Bugnini."

Three following pages held accompanying testimonies as to the veracity of the documents.

When Pope John Paul finished reading, he looked to Gagnon with stark seriousness: "How did we come by these documents?" "Both were obtained through Their Eminences, Cardinals Dino Staffa and Silvio Oddi. Cardinal Staffa died last year. But in 1975, then-Deputy Benelli contacted me and asked that I meet with Staffa in person. I did, of course, and listened to all the good man had to say. Even before Cardinal Staffa contacted Benelli about this material, he had asked special agents from Interpol to investigate these documents. They reported back that the documents were authentic. Cardinal Staffa, together with Cardinal Oddi, who had been conducting his own investigation, took the documents to the Holy Father. Certainly, Cardinal Benelli can give you a much more detailed report of the entire matter, should you wish. He, not Cardinal Villot, was present at that meeting with Pope Paul VI, Staffa and Oddi."

"Freemason bishops?" John Paul muttered, "You are a canon lawyer...," he looked to Gagnon, but did not finish his thought. He did not have to; the archbishop finished it for him.

"Any Catholic — lay or cleric — who enters Freemasonry, incurs automatic excommunication. Canon 2335," he quoted.

"Excommunication..." John Paul muttered the horrible-sounding word, "... to put the salvation of their souls in such..."

"As terrible as that is, Holy Father," Archbishop

Gagnon interjected, "far worse is the damage these two men have inflicted upon Christ's Church!"

"Archbishop Bugnini directed the liturgical reforms after the Council, going far beyond the mandate of the Council Fathers, in effect creating new liturgical and sacramental rites. He welcomed Protestant scholars to take part in his "renewal" of the Roman liturgy, a renewal that seems rather to be a reinvention. Liturgical "experimentation" has been rampant, making a plaything of the most solemn rites of the Church. And he presided over this revolution."

"We are aware." the pope said quietly. "But Archbishop Bugnini has been removed," he rather weakly added.

True enough; Bishop Annibale Bugnini, former Secretary of Sacred Congregation for Worship, and proud architect of the [1969] Novus Ordo Missae, the so-called "New Mass," had already been dealt with — technically, that is.

"As for Cardinal Baggio, Your Holiness," Gagnon pushed forward, "Here you have another very dangerous man championing Masonic ideals. No, no, Holy Father," Gagnon made an abrupt stop, "Not a 'very dangerous man championing Masonic ideals' - No! As the evidence demonstrates, a bishop who, because of his association with Freemasonry is de facto excommunicated -- and he continues to vet and nominate every Catholic bishop in the world!"

The gravity of allowing Sebastiano Baggio, cardinal and Freemason, to continue as Prefect of the Sacred Congregation for Bishops was simply and completely intolerable. Almost singlehandedly, "Brother Sebastiano," as he was addressed in the documentation, had chosen Catholic leaders worldwide since 1973.

Finally, Pope John Paul broke his long and thoughtful silence:

"You know, Excellency, Cardinal Benelli insists I confront Baggio. He says the only way to rid yourself of a vulture is to show him a higher perch."

"I don't know that I follow you, Holy Father."

"Cardinal Benelli suggests I appoint Baggio to Venice."

Édouard Gagnon's surprise showed, "Venice?! To try and fill your shoes? You say this is Cardinal Benelli's suggestion?"

"He says it's the only way Cardinal Baggio will go quietly. Given all the years of background checks, reports, and personal files about priests and bishops that have come into the Prefect's hands for the purpose of nominating bishops, Cardinal Benelli is concerned that his brother cardinal is in a unique position to blackmail any number of important and key people."

"Are you asking my opinion about that suggestion, Holy Father?"

"I am. You know what we're facing. You know the man. You know the delicacy of the situation."

After a moment's consideration, Archbishop Édouard Gagnon spoke with measured reservation: "If Cardinal Benelli says 'Send him to Venice!' then I would send him to Venice. Furthermore, if Cardinal Benelli were to tell me that I confront the man myself and hand him his walking papers, then I would tell him where to go — and the fastest way to get there. In other words, Most Holy Father: You, Pope John Paul, must confront the evil in person; You, Pope John Paul, must rid Rome of the evil."

"That, my dear Brother, is exactly what we feared you would say," he responded, managing to muster only a half-smile. "God be merciful," he added quietly.

"Is Your Holiness ready for a change of venue?" Gagnon asked, "The world of Vatican finances awaits. I should warn you, Holy Father, this, like everything else, also requires your urgent attention… I must further warn you that Vatican finances, like just about everything else I've come across these past few years, it is not unrelated to Freemasonry. In fact, they have had quite a stranglehold on the Church."

"Is it any wonder, dear Brother, that our predecessor of happy memory recoiled from hearing all of this?"

"The truth is, Holy Father, you've inherited a Church in terrible disarray. While the situation is dire, it can and must be addressed now. I have every hope that Your Holiness, with Cardinal Benelli as Secretary of State to assist you, can deal with this. There's still time. It can be done."

"God help us," the Pope prayed.

"Shall we continue, Your Holiness?"

About ten minutes after the Angelus, I heard: "Monsignore!" and looked up from my book to see a policeman waving in my direction. "His Excellency has arrived." There was Archbishop Édouard Gagnon making his way toward me. Even from a distance I saw the smile on his face. I jumped out and ran around to open the door for him. I took his much thinner and lighter book bag from him, this time without a word of protest from him.

No sooner had I retaken my place behind the wheel when I looked at him and asked point blank in Spanish: "Y?!" [And?!]

"We have much to be thankful for! The Almighty has seen fit to send us the right man for these trying times. You ask how it went, Don Carlo?" he repeated and smiled broadly as we made our way downhill around the basilica, "I'll tell you: the Holy Father himself and the audience were more than I had dared to hope for. And, believe me, regarding this entire matter and this very important audience with the new pope, I dared to hope very high! The mutual trust was immediate - almost palpable. I answered every question he had as clearly as I knew how. He listened with more than his ears, my boy; he listened with his heart; he listened with his Catholic soul."

"Wow!" I exclaimed, "It went that well?"

"Believe me; yes."

"What kind of a man is he, the new pope?"

"Santo y sabio [Saintly and wise]," he answered and nodding, agreed with himself, "There's no doubt about it," he continued, "Pope John Paul and Cardinal Giovanni Benelli are exactly what the Church militant has been waiting and praying for for two decades. They stand to outshine Sarto [Saint Pope Pius X] and Merry del Val [Pius X's talented and able Secretary of State.]"

Never had I seen Archbishop Édouard Joseph Gagnon so exultant, so absolutely pleased with life. He almost radiated contentment.

"The stranglehold on the Congregation for Bishops is about to be released." He then turned and looked at me. "You know, I almost feel sorry for Bugnini."

"Sorry? For Bugnini?!" I gave a kneejerk answer, "What would make you feel sorry for that lout?"

"What a tragedy for a man to lose his soul; for him to forfeit his soul. And for what? I'll never understand it. At least, I hope I never do." He looked out the side window and spoke softer, to himself, "And from so far a distance, to have to watch what he sold his soul for crumble and disintegrate."

It seemed clear to me that the distance of which he spoke was much, much further than that between Rome and Teheran.

Of course, the accomplishments of the day called for at least a minor celebration, and later that evening, Gagnon, Marini and I, drove to the Twelve Apostles Bar and Pizzeria, in Piazza dei Dodici Apostoli.

Gagnon did not go into details about his special audience with the Pope, other than to declare it "tremendously successful," to which he also added, to cover his bases: "So far."

After the first major "salute" to "His Holiness, Pope John Paul," Mario Marini asked rather bluntly: "Did you mention my case to the pope?"

Édouard Gagnon put down his glass stein, looked at him and said: "I had a decision to make this morning. Either I helped map out the future of the Roman Catholic Church with the Vicar of Christ on earth, whose precious, full and focused attention I had for a very limited period of time, OR I took that time to explain to Christ's Vicar the unfair plight of Monsignor Mario Marini.

"I chose the former — for which, my friend, I do not apologize— especially knowing, as do you, that your case will be resolved soon enough, when the pope names his new Secretary of State.

"We must all learn to be patient, Mario," he said and lifted his stein, "The time and the place and the right man are just around the corner," he said and added a second toast of the evening: "To His Eminence, Cardinal Giovanni Benelli!"

"And to patience," I dared to add.

"GOOD NIGHT, HOLY FATHER"

September 28, 1978

Albino Luciani had always been a man of prayer. Long before his ordination to priesthood he had disciplined himself to begin each day with Divine Office and meditation. After ordination in 1935, that "dawn of prayer" was usually followed by Mass.

This morning, seated before the Tabernacle in the silent tranquility of his private chapel, Pope John Paul could not keep his mind focused nor his thoughts organized. An interior battle with tens of recurring scrimmages invaded his every pious intention.

Giovanni Benelli's invaluable experience, his heartfelt motivational talks, his clear directions, together with Édouard Gagnon's detailed Curial investigation results, personal observations and encouragement to forge ahead, undoubtedly strengthened the pope's determination. Still, the nearer that dreaded face-to-face encounter with Cardinal Sebastiano Baggio approached, the more his discomfort grew. This was the first definitive battle of his pontificate, and both Benelli and Gagnon had assured him it could be neither avoided nor postponed. Occasionally he took his eyes from the Tabernacle and Crucifix to consult his watch. Still twelve and a half hours of disquieting anticipation to endure.

At ten o'clock in the morning, the pope picked up the phone in his study and called the office of the Sacred Congregation for Bishops. Somewhat diffidently, he asked the desk clerk if Cardinal Sebastiano Baggio might be free to take his call. When asked who was calling, John Paul answered simply "il Papa." The nervous clerk barged in on his superior and a group of African bishops to inform him of the call.

Pope John Paul expressed his desire to meet with Baggio that same day. When the cardinal responded that his schedule was particularly heavy and asked if they could meet the next day, the Holy Father proposed to see him after office hours. "This evening then, in my study."

"As Your Holiness wishes," the Prefect agreed.

Just minutes before eight o'clock that evening, a loud knock on the doors to the Papal Apartments announced the cardinal's arrival. It was an unusual time of day for a meeting, and unusual as well that no one else was to be present. The Swiss Guards were told to expect him. The door opened, and Cardinal Baggio went in.

The two men, arguably the most powerful figures in the Catholic Church, faced each other across the desk. The tension was palpable. The urgency of the appointment, and the fact that the pope would not even put it off for even one day, suggested to Cardinal Baggio that a moment of reckoning had come. Archbishop Gagnon and his black book bag, bulging with documentation from his three years' intense investigation, was very much on the cardinal's mind. He had been accused of ties with Freemasonry during the pontificate of Paul VI, and had categorically and vigorously denied the accusation. But this was a different pope, not a man with whom he had worked for many years. An outsider, the new pope was free of both the loyalties and jealousies that abounded in curial circles. And he had seen Gagnon's just days before. How would this new occupant of the Chair of Peter approach him?

The Holy Father had his own reasons for trepidation. By nature a conciliatory man, he was now confronting — so early in his pontificate! — an emotional and unnerving situation. The man across from him was one of the

Sebastiano Cardinal Baggio

highest-ranking members of the Roman Curia, a bishop who had given many years of service to the Holy See. How Papa Luciani dealt with the serious charges he had heard about him would send reverberations through the whole Curia. No matter what path he chose, his action would instantly make friends or foes of many. And, if Cardinal Benelli was to be believed, the cardinal would resist efforts to be removed and could be ruthless in defending his position. The gravity of the evidence made it plain that something substantive must be done now, immediately. The scandal had already simmered far too long. All day long, the Holy Father had felt the anguish of this encounter in the depths of his soul. How tempting it would have been to put it off, even for a day, as the Prefect had suggested. But, having made his decision, the pope was resolved to act quickly, lest his courage desert him.

The meeting lasted about forty-five minutes. No one else was present, and the only testimony about it came via the grapevine in the days after — the Swiss Guards on duty later reported that voices were raised, suggesting that it was very contentious. No one apart from Cardinal Baggio knew what was said, or what thoughts filled his mind as he closed the door.

⁓

Even with one eye half-opened, I could see that it was the middle of the night. I turned over, intent on getting back to sleep. The knocking at my door started up again.

"Chi è? Cosa c'è?" I called out.

Whoever was on the other side of my door was knocking so hard, rapidly and incessantly, that he could not hear me calling out and asking who it was and what he wanted.

"Charlie! It's me: Fernando! Open!"

Seriously annoyed — the outlandish disturbance must have awakened the entire residence— nevertheless, I opened and my Costa Rican friend and classmate entered. Suddenly, I was more confused than irritated. This made no sense. Luis Fernando Soto lived across town, on the other side of the Tiber, at San Anselmo on the Aventine hill. What was he doing here, and at this hour? Strategically speaking: How did he get past our three lines of defense: the Syrians, the Israelis, and — fiercest of all when provoked before breakfast — the Lebanese nuns?

At any rate, there stood Luis Fernando, in a state of shock.

"All right! Calm down! What is so earth-shakingly important? What?! Did the pope die?!" I asked this just to illustrate what I meant by "earthshaking".

I watched Luis Fernando's jaw drop and his previously startled eyes widen even further.

"You mean, you already knew?" he asked with incredulous amazement, "How?"

I was completely awake now and did not find Fernando's antics in the least bit amusing. "What do you mean, how?! Did it take that news a month to reach the Aventine?"

"Charlie, I just came from Mass at Saint Peter's: the pope, the new pope, Pope John Paul: He's dead, Charlie! Turn on Radio Vaticana and hear it for yourself."

I turned on the Grundig and fine-tuned the channel until I heard clearly a male voice solemnly confirming Luis Fernando's claim.

"They killed him," the shaken Costa Rican said, "They murdered the pope!"

One quick rap on my open door revealed an unhappy and growling Mario Marini. "You're making enough noise in here to raise the dead! What in the world is going on here?"

"Basta! Come in and listen to this!" I ordered and turned up the radio volume a notch. The male announcer repeated in Italian: "After a thirty-four-day pontificate, the Holy Father, Pope John Paul, is dead..." In the background, the deepest bell of the basilica slowly tolled the pontiff's sixty-six years on earth. Mario Marini collapsed into my reading chair. He made the sign of the cross and listened carefully to every word of the radio commentary.

I hurried down the cold marble floor barefoot to inform our two other third-floor residents. I knocked first on Archbishop Gagnon's door and, immediately after on Archbishop Capucci's. Within a second of each other, both doors opened and two wondering gazes stared at me. From the corridor, in French, I announced the alarming news.

"Mais, tu as fait un cauchemar, Père Charles!" Capucci remarked.

"A nightmare, to be sure, Excellency; but not mine alone. The Holy Father is dead. Turn on Vatican Radio."

Then, in a Spanish aside, I told Édouard Gagnon that Mario Marini and I were in my room and that he should join us.

"Voy," he answered.

"Gagnon's on his way," I told Marini as soon as I reentered my room. Calling my Costa Rican friend aside, I asked him to go to the café around the corner to get four caffé lattes and cornetti.

No sooner had the seminarian left when the archbishop arrived. I gave Édouard Gagnon my desk chair and I sat on the corner of the bed. For ten solid minutes, the three of us listened to the radio with rapt attention. It seemed surreal: could we really be hearing this? One thing was for sure, the vigor with which Archbishop Gagnon was shaking his head made it clear that he was not buying the simple "heart attack" explanation. When it was reported that the pontiff was found in a serene, sleeping position holding a copy of The Imitation of Christ in his lifeless hands that proved too much for both my early-morning guests.

"It's like most things they touch …," Archbishop Gagnon angrily muttered. He did not finish the sentence. He didn't have to. It was plain to see that this death hit him extremely hard.

"Filthy Masons!" Mario Marini spat the words out.

While not disagreeing with him, Gagnon looked at both of us and suggested, "Let us offer a prayer for the repose of his soul."

We stood and with ancient Latin orations we implored heaven's mercy on the soul of our departed pontiff and on our own as well. As always, Archbishop Gagnon offered our prayers to the Triune God, through the intercession of the Blessed Virgin. Just before he ended, he stopped and invited Mario and me to invoke with him a powerful heavenly figure. Intensely, with his eyes pressed tightly closed, he began: "Sancte Michael Archangele… [Saint Michael the archangel, defend us in battle, be our defense against the wickedness and snares of the devil. May God rebuke him, we humbly pray, and you, O prince of the heavenly host, by the power of God, thrust into hell Satan and all the evil spirits who roam about the world seeking the ruin of souls. Amen".]

A STROLL IN THE GARDEN

October 8, 1978

The approaching conclave was having a positive effect on my friend Mario: his complaints regarding his dismissal from the Secretariat of State, his rants against Cardinal Jean Villot for that grave injustice, and his lamentations over his relocation from the center of things to the Jesuit Prep School in EUR had lessened considerably. My mentor's attention had returned to the much bigger picture.

Marini was speaking to Archbishop Gagnon, "Well, Monsignore, having had quite an extraordinary dress rehearsal, the surviving cardinals will meet again on the fourteenth."

"Yes, this Saturday," I observed, content to add something, however meager, to the conversation of these two "above and beyond" savvy gentlemen.

As we were to meet Monsignor Zannoni for dinner later on that evening, the three of us decided to forego pranzo and take full advantage of the crisp autumn weather and the midday quiet of a Roman Sunday for a long walk in the gardens of Villa Schiarra.

Of course, I marveled to myself how these two men already knew — or seemed to know— or thought they knew - the identity of the next pope. They spoke of a man I had never heard of; a cardinal from Poland! How absurd, I thought, a Polish pope.

However, I clearly recalled the Ravenna/Mexico phone call in which Mario named that "next pope," Albino Luciani, albeit in "Saint Malachy code." On that occasion, he also spoke of a non-Italian possibility. Could this man be him? My friends were predicting that in just a matter of days, that foreign candidate would be elected. "In fact," Gagnon told us, "Cardinal Karol Wojtyla is Benelli's candidate. I believe he would make a good pope."

"With Benelli as his Secretary of State," Marini jumped right in, "How could he not make a good pope?"

"And Benelli?" I asked, "Couldn't he win the election himself?"

"Well…"

"I can tell you this much," Édouard Gagnon responded, "Cardinal Benelli possesses two outstanding qualities — two that outshine his many others. They are honesty and pragmatism.

"And determination," Mario could not resist adding, "The man has a will of steel."

"Because of these," Gagnon continued, "nothing in the August conclave got past him unnoticed. Not a thing." He pursed his lips and nodded his head in a sort of wondering admiration for the man, "Again, because he is honest and pragmatic and determined," he gave an acquiescent nod to Mario, "Benelli entered the last conclave knowing he would not be elected. He went in with one major objective in mind: to prevent the leadership of the Catholic Church from being usurped by a Freemason who, if elected pope, would oversee the ruination of the Church."

The statement almost knocked me over.

A moment of silence passed.

"You know, I heard Cardinal Baggio interviewed on Vatican Radio the day after the pope's death," I said. "They wanted his reaction to the news. His answer: 'Che colpo.' [What a blow.] When the same reporter interviewed the Archbishop of Milan, Cardinal Colombo, he had answered: 'I spoke with him only a few days ago and he sounded wonderful, in good health,' or words to that effect. But when they asked Baggio, the last person to see him alive, all he could get out were two words: 'Che colpo.'

Both of my companions nodded matter-of-factly. We sat on a bench to survey the gardens.

I decided to stir things up a bit, and so went on: "You know, Mario, the Vatican just released another statement, a 'clarification,' that Papa Luciani died of a heart attack." I stated this with obvious skepticism.

My friend rose to the bait: "Villot and Casaroli have been saying that, or versions of it, from the beginning. It's the embellishments around the heart attack that keep changing. They can't keep their stories straight. They should just sit down and agree on one story, and then stick to the script!"

He continued, "From the very beginning, didn't I say what pure codswallop that was about Papa Luciani dying in bed while reading The Imitation of Christ? I told you: poisonings or heart attacks leave the victim's body convulsed — not slumbering in peace, with reading-glasses neatly in place, and both hands holding an open book..."

I watched Édouard Gagnon's expression. He was not disagreeing with what he was hearing.

"If he was reading anything," Marini went on, "it was a list of urgent changes he had to make in the Roman Curia! Why, it could have been Monsignore's own list!" he said, acknowledging Édouard Gagnon's efforts in the urgent cause of Curial reform. My friend was now getting worked up: "And that in this day and age the Frenchman [Villot] refused to authorize an autopsy of the Vicar of Christ - the spiritual leader of over half a billion Catholics, a man all the world suspects was murdered by his own den of vipers - is one of the most outrageous and audacious things I've ever heard in my life! And, believe me," he lifted his open hand as if swearing an oath, "When it comes to outrageous and audacious, I've heard enough for three lifetimes!"

I waited for Mario Marini to cool down before I asked Archbishop Gagnon: "And you, Excellency, do you think Papa Luciani's death involved foul play?" I wanted to ask, "Do you think the pope was murdered?" but I wasn't comfortable being so blunt about it.

He was slow to answer. I could see how seriously he considered my question. He knew that I had asked it in all sincerity. Did he consider me too young to handle the truth of it? Was he looking for a way to answer honestly without scandalizing me?

He stood, dusted off the seat of his black pants, and we resumed our walk.

The crunching of the gravel underfoot exaggerated the stark silence.

"There are any number of ways a man might be killed," he finally said, "You'd agree with me so far, no?"

"Absolutely," I eagerly granted.

"Would you also agree that -" he stopped in midsentence, "Let me be very clear," he warned, "We're speaking here theoretically. Is that understood?"

The faint smirk he had on his face and the way his eyebrows were raised seemed to tell me — and, I believed, Mario, as well - that what he was about to say was just a tad beyond theoretical.

"Understood," I affirmed.

"First off: all this street-talk," he shook his head, "rumors of tea-poisoning or of pillow strangulation ... such things are out of the question. But he could have died because those around him did not urge him to attend to matters relating to his health. In such a case, the Holy Father's death could be the result of incompetence or neglect." He pressed on: "If, in fact, there really was 'foul play' in this case, then I do not find it unreasonable to entertain the possibility of a sixty-six-year-old man being induced

— pushed, if you will, beyond his physical and emotional limits - into cardiac arrest."

"Particularly when that sixty-six-year-old has a weak heart, a history of coronary problems, and is taking prescribed heart medications," Mario added.

"The point I'm trying to make is this," Gagnon went on, "You ask if I suspect 'foul play' in the death of Pope John Paul. If by that you mean: do I believe he was murdered, the answer must be, 'no.' Do I think he was killed indirectly — then, my answer is, 'yes,' I do believe he might have been."

Mario picked up the question from there: "Cardinal Villot claims he was the last person to see the Holy Father alive. The Frenchman is covering for his friend. The real 'last person' to see the Holy Father alive was none other than Sebastiano Baggio. Baggio, who argued with the pope so heatedly that the Swiss Guards heard his yelling in the outside corridor! Baggio, who I've heard told the pope to his face that he refused, flatly refused, to leave the Vatican, even after the pope offered him Venice! Wouldn't treatment like that frighten half to death a humble, timid man with the weight of the world on his shoulders?"

"Hmmm...," I mused to myself, "... murder in the thirty-third degree?"

"Sorry?" Gagnon asked. "Never mind."

I tried not to show it, but my friends' words stunned me. It was one thing to hear such things bruited about on Roman street corners by ordinary people who have a taste for gossip and scandal, quite another to hear them from highly-placed Churchmen, and especially from these two, whose insight and wisdom I regarded so highly.

A series of questions raced through my mind. Why didn't the Holy Father summon guards and have the shouting, wrought-up cardinal escorted from his room? What evidence concerning Cardinal Baggio had my friend presented to the pope, and what effect would the confirmation of such serious charges against one the most highly-placed men in the Vatican have had on him?

My thoughts drifted from Baggio to Archbishop Bugnini. It was common knowledge that his "promotion" to Iran by Pope Paul had in fact meant dismissal and exile. And yet it was Pope Paul himself who had brought the liturgical expert back from exile! Annibale Bugnini had served as an advisor during the pontificate of Pius XII, but "good Pope John" sent him packing. Papa Montini reinstated him. And then he allowed him to direct the implementation of the liturgical reforms mandated by the Council Fathers, reforms that went far beyond what they had asked for or imagined. I remembered vividly one very disturbing exchange I had with Monsignor Marini. I asked him: "In other words, the new Mass, the Novus Ordo, was created by a Freemason, an excommunicate who, if he dies unrepentant, will appear before God already damned to hell?" And he pointedly answered, "No, not 'in other words' — those are the very words!"

The evidence seemed conclusive that both Archbishop Bugnini and Cardinal Baggio were Freemasons. In accord with Church law at the time, this meant that in fact they were automatically excommunicated. How could this state of affairs have been allowed to go on for so long … and in the case of Cardinal Baggio, this was still the case. Prelates? They were excommunicated Catholics.

My thoughts flitted from the past and present to the future. Clearly, whether it was Benelli's Polish candidate or some other who was elected, this mess had to be dealt with once and for all. I was not alone in my silent thoughts: Archbishop Gagnon, too, was pensive and silent, with the kind of silence mourners observe at a graveside.

FROM A DISTANT COUNTRY

October 16, 1978

Two days before the second conclave of 1978, I drove over toward the Vatican after my morning classes at the Gregorian University. Just before the Via della Conciliazione arrives at St. Peter's Square, there's a short, narrow side street: Via Padre Pancrazio Pfeiffer. Named for the Bavarian priest who saved hundreds of Jews during the German occupation in 1943, the modest alley was easily overlooked — and, as such, it never failed to provide me with a secret parking spot. The bonus today was that it was next door to my favorite bookstore. There I met up with a priest friend who worked there, one of my favorite people in Rome.

Born in Bergamo and seven years my senior, Carlo Bertola was a member of the religious community responsible for this store, and he had asked my help in organizing its English book section. Carlo was a true human rarity: he was naturally good — that is, good by nature. He was the kind of man that - as my French Great-Grandmother used to say — "Le bon Dieu n'en fait qu'un, chaque vingt-neuf février, [The good Lord makes only one, and only every leap year]." So, when my Bergamasco brother asked a favor of me, I always did my best to oblige.

We rolled up our sleeves and began tackling the problem facing us. Since just about all of the three-thousand books in English had been shelved haphazardly, step one was to remove them all from the bookcases and place them on the ground, to be classified and categorized later. Younger and (presumably) nimbler, I was elected to climb the ladder and lower each of the dusty volumes to Nico, our "acrophobic" assistant. Rolling the library ladder to the fifth bookshelf, I made my ascent; from this perch, as I turned to hand more books to Nico, I thought I saw someone I knew.

"Hey!" quietly but loudly enough I called to Carlo Bertola.

He looked up at me from the nearby register where he was with a customer, smiled, and gave a "What's up?" jerk of the head.

"Identification: eleven o'clock."

Carlo turned slightly to the left, to the Latin Missal and Breviary section, took one look at the stocky man in cassock, double-breasted coat and round black saturno hat, and announced: "Si, Signore."

I quickly climbed down, wiped my hands on a towel, and walked over to pay my respects to Cardinal Pericles Felici, the President of the Pontifical Commission for the Revision of the Code of Canon Law. Coincidentally, this was the first Roman clergyman I had ever met, right outside this very bookstore, when I was seventeen.

"Laudetur Jesus Christus," I greeted him.

"Nunc et usque in aeternum," the cardinal responded, even before turning to see who it was. But, when he did turn and to see, the smile was immediate, full and real.

"Charlie!" he exclaimed, "Just a moment ago," he pointed upward and rightward, "was that you up there?"

I apologized for my appearance. He was used to seeing me in cassock, starched Roman collar, and black leather shoes — but for this cleaning assignment I was wearing jeans and a sweatshirt. He completely understood (or said he did) and laughed (or, at least, chuckled) it off.

"I still haven't gotten over your ordination," he declared.

"Yes," I willingly concurred, "Beautiful, wasn't it? Your Eminence and Archbishop Gagnon helped make it..."

"Beautiful, most certainly," he interrupted, "but I was referring to the physical nightmare of getting to the church!" He remembered, shook his head, looked heavenward, and sighed, "...Madonna Santa! What a day, that day! Student rioters... Delinquenti! Teppisti! [Criminals! Thugs!] They were protesting the death of a Roman student, 'Valter' Something-or-other. The mob engulfed our car! They were rocking it and shouting. Had it not been for Monsignor Marini's quick thinking and bravery, I don't know how it would have ended! This made us arrive five minutes late. Everyone waiting for us, ... Me, the only Italian I know who arrives ten minutes early for everything! Gagnon would have had to proceed without us. I still don't know how I got through the Mass and ordination."

"Do you know," he added pensively, "I learned something that day. When you see and hear Communist thugs conglomerating and yelling at the top of their lungs: 'VALTER VIVE! VALTER VIVE!! VIVA VALTER!!!' [WALTER LIVES! WALTER LIVES!! LONG LIVE WALTER!!!]" he discreetly imitated the protesters' cries, "you can deduce one thing, and one thing only."

"And that is?" I took the bait.

"That whoever Valter once was, now Valter is dead!"

Of course, with the death of Pope John Paul fresh in everyone's mind, we spoke about his brief pontificate.

"Speaking of brief, Eminence," I segued, "the day after the Holy Father died Vatican Radio transmitted the briefest interview I have ever heard. Until then, I considered 'nessun commento' [no comment] the shortest brush-off anyone could give to an annoying reporter. But 'Che colpo!' [What a blow!] beats that by ...," I stopped and did a rapid finger tally, "... by six letters! That 'brief' comment had to be a record-breaker!"

"A major figure? And that's all he had to say?" Felici wondered.

"Yes," I continued, "and as he was the last person to see and speak with the Holy Father, you'd think he'd have more than two measly words to share with a world in shock."

The smile on Felici's usually amiable face evaporated. With unobtrusive but definite force he took me by the arm and guided me to the furthest corner of the bookstore.

"How do you know this?" he demanded.

"I heard it myself. Those two exact words where the full extent of His Eminence, Cardinal Baggio's interview on Radio Vaticana," I answered.

"No, no, not that," he said dismissively, "that the person interviewed…"

"Cardinal Baggio," I affirmed.

"Yes, him. That he was the last to see and speak with the Holy Father. How do you know that?"

I excused myself, walked over to Carlo's register and took a magazine from the lower shelf. I returned, magazine in hand, to the waiting cardinal, opened TIME to page sixty-eight, and pointed to the second paragraph in column two.

Cardinal Felici read it without commenting.

"Ma!" he finally grumbled, "What importance can we give the press, today?" he seemed to dismiss TIME's claim that "on that evening, [i.e, the pope's last on earth] Cardinal Sebastiano Baggio, Prefect for the Sacred Congregation for Bishops, was summoned by the pope to discuss pressing business." (No other publication recorded that detail.)

As we ended our conversation, it occurred to me that Cardinal Felici was the man who would announce the name of the new pope after the conclave. Recalling the papal candidate that Giovanni Benelli had pinned his hopes on, and that Cardinal Felici had pronounced the student's

Pericle Cardinal Felici

name as "Valter", I was tempted to say: "Remember now: the 'W' in Polish is pronounced the same as the 'V' in Latin; 'V', as in 'WALTER."

But I did not.

❦

"Il fumo bianco! Fumo bi-an-co! [White smoke!]" Monsignor Marini screamed in my ear. It was the evening of October 16, the second day of the conclave.

I grabbed my binoculars, jumped into my car, zipped down the Gianicolo, and made my way to St. Peter's Square. As one in this crowd of some two hundred thousand from every part of the world, I felt as I sensed each of them did: proudly Catholic and absolutely at home in this sea of people who did not know one another but felt more like family than like strangers. I stood near the colossal statue of St. Peter clutching his keys, anxiously waiting to learn the identity of his latest successor.

Early that very morning, while Gagnon, Marini, and I vested for Mass, the archbishop had invited us to keep the success of the conclave in our intentions.

"I pray for the election every day," I told him honestly, "that God's will be done." "The will of God. By all means...," Gagnon replied with the tone of an understanding father, "... the will of God. But given the circumstances, would it hurt to be a little bit more specific? Everyone wants God's will to be done. Should we not pray, then, for our friend, a man with the intelligence and courage to see that it will be?"

"Cardinal Benelli?" I inquired needlessly.

"Yes," Gagnon answered me, "May his candidate be in complete conformity to God's holy will," Gagnon said and blessed himself.

"And may our will be God's," Marini whispered to me and concluded with a solid "Amen."

As we celebrated the holy sacrifice of the Mass, each of us silently offered the intentions dearest to our hearts. I am sure Édouard Gagnon prayed for the day to arrive when he could sit down with the new pope and present his final investigative report. And, as a man specific in his upward pleadings, he probably prayed that the reform of the Vatican be done properly, under the direct supervision of its new Secretary of State, Cardinal Giovanni Benelli.

No doubt Mario Marini's private prayer was for his swift reinstatement in the Vatican Secretariat. He had reason to be hopeful that this would come to pass if Giovanni Benelli replaced Jean Villot as Secretary of State.

My prayer for myself was insignificant compared to those of my seniors: I prayed to finish my doctorate successfully. I also considered my prayer much easier to answer than theirs: mine did not require the intervention of Cardinal Giovanni Benelli!

My thoughts returned to the present moment as I stood waiting with the crowd. Evening gave way to night and powerful spotlights aimed at the balcony gave a forceful air of drama to what was unfolding. As the curtains up in the loggia were pulled back, I raised my binoculars to watch every magnified movement of this larger-than-life moment.

The huge glass-paneled doors of the basilica's central balcony opened fully to reveal a glimmering processional cross emerging, held high by a nervous young acolyte. Behind the cross, a trio of acolytes appeared around Cardinal Pericles Felici. Before he pronounced the formulaic words that everyone waited anxiously to hear, he looked out over the immense crowd, obviously moved by the sight, and seemed to be studying it.

He read from the large, red-covered Caeremoniale:

"Annuntio vobis gaudium magnum...," he declared, and immediately the crowd exploded into wild applause and cries of "Viva il Papa!!"

Again, the stocky cardinal studied the sea of humanity before him, as if attempting to etch this magnificent moment in his memory and keep it alive forever. I saw it in his expression and heard it in his voice. He seemed acutely aware of the singular honor bestowed upon him at this moment in history.

"...Habemus Papam!" he picked up where he had left off.

The crowd went even wilder, with louder cheers, and more thunderous applause! Felici continued: "... Eminentissimum ac reverendissimum Dominum... Carolum...

"'V' as in 'Walter', Eminence," I smiled and said to myself.

"Who did he say?!" a woman loudly asked anyone who might know.

"...Sanctae Romanae Ecclesiae, Cardinalem Wojtyla."

"Wojtyla?!" was the name on the lips of two hundred thousand people around me, and God only knew how many hundreds of millions more throughout the world.

There was general confusion as to just who this new pontiff could be.

"Africain? Un pape africain!" exclaimed a French couple directly behind me.

I turned and offered a friendly correction: "Pas africain," I said, "Polonais. De Cracovie. De Pologne," I repeated this, but apparently left them both unconvinced.

People continued streaming into the Square, the crowd now numbering well over two hundred thousand. Many hugged, some - perhaps Polish or from Eastern Bloc countries - cried, others waved white handkerchiefs, some children and teenagers actually jumped for joy, one couple kissed.

"Blessed be God," I said to myself, half in prayer, half sighing with relief.

Although I had been told repeatedly by my friends that Cardinal Benelli's candidate, Karol Józef Wojtyla, would be elected, until this moment, when I heard Cardinal Felici announce the Polish cardinal's name from the balcony of Saint Peter's Basilica, I was not one-hundred percent convinced.

Within minutes, Karl Wojtyla, who had taken his predecessor's name, John Paul, appeared for the first time as pope. The cheering and applauding grew and grew. Without a doubt Pope John Paul the Second's short introductory discourse from the balcony endeared him to countless millions.

It was time to hurry back home and toast the new pontiff with a shot of Archbishop Gagnon's Colombian aguardiente.

I drove as fast as I could, all the way anticipating the smiles, congratulatory abrazos, and maybe even a tear or two, from my friends and brothers, Édouard Gagnon and Mario Marini. Could Archbishop Gagnon expect a telephone call that very night?

THE ARCHBISHOP ACTS

January 15, 1979

Christmastide had come and gone. In fact, we were two weeks into the new year, 1979; three months, to the day, into the Wojtyla pontificate, and yet Archbishop Gagnon had not been called to present his Roman Curia investigation results. This, in spite of various attempts by Cardinal Giovanni Benelli to procure a meeting between the Pope and the Archbishop.

When Pope John Paul II reconfirmed Archbishop Édouard Gagnon as President of the Pontifical Committee for the Family, he sent word to him that he looked forward to a private meeting with him "to discuss important affairs of State." The meeting, however, would have to wait until after his return from Mexico — after February first.

I considered this good news, but no one else, including Archbishop Édouard Gagnon, shared my optimism. And while the Holy Father's confirmation of Gagnon as President of the Pontifical Committee for the Family was very good news, the very bad news was that the new pope had reconfirmed everyone else in the Roman Curia to the very same position he had under Pope Paul VI. In other words, Cardinal Sebastiano Baggio was still in charge of the world's bishops, and his friend, Cardinal Jean Villot, remained Vatican Secretary of State.

It was around this time that I decided to arrange a dinner in honor of Archbishop Gagnon on his sixty-first birthday. I picked a place to lift our spirits, at least for a few hours: Fantasie di Trastevere. Monsignor Marini demurred: "First of all, even if Gagnon agrees, you're not dragging me into a

Saint Pope John Paul II

Trastevere cabaret for the night!" I made a sour face, "What 'cabaret?' Fantasie is a fine old theater from the 1800's, converted into a restaurant with great food and a 'musical revue'. And the music and singing are outstanding."

"And the women half-naked," he objected.

It took me a minute to stop laughing.

"Listen, I went there once with some American friends. The youngest woman I remember on stage was a soprano in her early forties. I think you're man enough to handle the temptation," I said and started laughing again. "It's mostly Italian music from the 30's and 40's — with an occasional tenor singing a piece from the belle époque." All of the sudden, Marini thought Fantasie was a great idea.

When we arrived on Sunday evening, January 14, 1979, the proprietor escorted us to a secluded balcony, stage left. We could speak freely there. It was plain to see that both my friends liked the place — a lot.

"I invited Zannoni and Lobina," I said as soon as we were seated.

"Let me guess," Mario put both elbows on the table and pretended to ponder for a moment. "Lobina said, 'I have too much work to do on Mario's legal case,'" my friend said in Sardinian-accented Italian, "'besides, I have an early morning lecture to deliver at the Laterano, and must be my brilliant self; my students demand it of me!'" Gagnon and I laughed at his imitation of the lawyer. "Zannoni, on the other hand, told you that it was too late at night for him, that he retires early — while the truth of it is, he never goes anywhere where he might feel uncomfortable in cassock and collar."

Of course, Mario was absolutely correct in both cases, and we all shared a good laugh. "Regardless," I said, "They both send birthday greetings and prayers your way, Monseigneur." "Good men, both of them," Gagnon said with the satisfaction of a man blessed in his friendships. "Zannoni is the real deal, a true saint. God bless him."

"So that leaves us," Mario said as he filled our glasses with the deep red of Montepulciano. "To you, Monsignore," Mario began the toast and we raised our glasses, "For all you have given to His Church, and all you have done for her over your lifetime. May God reward you a hundredfold in this life and grant you heaven forever after. And to our friendships," he added and gave each of us an individual nod of acknowledgement, "God's greatest gift to us mere mortals! Happy birthday!"

After several minutes of small talk, I took a sip of wine, cleared my voice and blurted out: "Speaking of Cardinal Benelli, has anyone heard from the good man lately?"

Mario Marini gave his "Gna, gna, gna," low-laugh, "You know, Monsignore," he looked Gagnon squarely in the eyes, "Questi Americani," he smiled, "It's what I've always admired about them; no standing on ceremony. No, signore! It's right down to business."

"Well, yes," Édouard Gagnon said, "I spoke with him just last Thursday. He's trying to arrange the audience with the pope, so I can deliver and explain the Visitation report."

"That's great news!" I exclaimed.

"It would have been great news," the archbishop qualified, "had it happened before the Holy Father told everyone to stay right where he was — in his same office, with his same job. And that meeting might have happened sooner had the Holy Father not reconfirmed Villot as his Secretary of State."

"Who can understand that move?" I asked.

"I can understand it," Gagnon said, "I don't agree with it, but I understand it."

"What do you mean, you understand it?" I asked.

Whenever Jean Villot was brought up, it unnerved Marini, but right now he was calm. "The Holy Father learned what Villot himself only learned a few weeks ago. Villot has inoperable lung cancer... The doctors give him less than six months. Casaroli's picking up the slack. He phoned me on Thursday to tell me that the audience will have to wait - until the pope returns from Mexico."

"And that will be?" I asked.

"The first of February," Mario answered at once.

"The first of February," Édouard Gagnon repeated cheerlessly. "I'm afraid of what Villot and Casaroli are planning..."

"You mean plotting," Mario corrected.

"I'm afraid of what they've got a mind to do, and very soon; a thing that would have far-reaching consequences."

"And that would be?" I asked.

"Convincing our new pope to make a smooth transition from Secretary of State Villot to Secretary of State Casaroli — sidestepping Benelli completely."

"God forbid such a calamity from happening," Marini shuddered at the thought of it. "Bad enough that the pope kept 'Brother Jean and Brother Sebastiano' in the first place," he declared, referring to their alleged Masonic associations, "But for the pope to let that man name his own successor is, is, well..." Knowing Mario, I realized he wasn't searching for the right word, but rather eliminating several words readily at his disposal out of respect for the Holy Father. "Well, ... it would be colossally imprudent."

"Imprudent?" I repeated and, without giving it a second, "more prudent," thought, I blurted out what Mario had certainly eliminated in his mental gymnastics: "Pendejez imperdonable! [Unpardonable stupidity]!"

"Excuse me, Monseigneur," Mario jumped in, "I agree with what Charlie's trying to say. You know better than anyone that Villot should have been thanked for his years of service to Montini, given a pat on the head and sent back to Lyons. Benelli should have taken the reins immediately

— day one of Papa Wojtyla's pontificate. Not only did the pope reconfirm every member of the corrupt Vatican government in his place, but now this?! That it's even being considered is beyond belief… You've got to get that audience with the pope before it's too late to do anything; before it's all lost."

An uncomfortable silence fell upon that table in the first balcony, stage left. Visibly upset, irritated, Archbishop Édouard Gagnon pursed his lips tightly and said nothing. I wasn't sure if it was because of my disrespectful remark or because he was being prevented from seeing the pope and presenting the investigation report in full. I had seen my Canadian friend like this once before. It was like watching an active volcano that by some miracle of nature did not erupt.

Then, a veritable godsend to break the tension. The entire ensemble of singers was front stage, center: soprano and tenor and eight men and women, began a full-throated rendition of La Romanina, then Quanto Sei Bella Roma, two of Gagnon's folkloric favorites. The final tension breaker arrived in the guise of a beautiful young lady descending from on high, seated on a swing, and clad in turn-of-the-century hat and dress, as La Romanina segued into La Spagnola. Singing was Gagnon's one delightful weakness. Both he and I knew the lyrics to the old Neapolitan song, and Marini knew better than to destroy the moment by attempting to join in.

While Édouard Joseph Gagnon was almost back to his old self - at least not half as perturbed as he had been twenty minutes previously — to get his thoughts off what we had managed getting them onto, Mario gave a brief progress report on his own plight and then began talking about a very interesting avenue that just might be open to him in his quest to have his case heard sometime this century.

"A mysterious, middle-aged woman showed up last

Friday at the Congregation for the Clergy and asked to speak with Monsignor Guglielmo Zannoni," Marini began, "Seems she — well, not really she herself, but a very close friend of hers -- had corresponded with Zannoni many years ago regarding a matter of great personal significance to the woman."

"And?" I encouraged that him to continue.

"Well, years ago her friend, a Polish doctor, married, with four children, had been diagnosed with cancer and given very little time to live. She had a very close friend, a young priest who had just been made auxiliary bishop of Cracow. Through a student priest in Rome at the time, Bishop Wojtyla discovered that Zannoni was a friend of Padre Pio of Pietrelcina."

"Our Monsignor Zannoni? He knew Padre Pio?"

"They were good friends," Gagnon said.

"Bishop Wojtyla wrote a letter to Padre Pio asking a miracle for this woman with a husband and four little children to care for. She was one of his dearest and closest friends in the world and he asked Padre Pio to storm heaven for this particular favor. Wojtyla sent the letter to Monsignor Zannoni and asked him to get it to Padre Pio as soon as possible and to make sure he read it. Zannoni in turn gave the letter to a friend of his, Archbishop Battisti, who was in charge of Padre Pio's hospital, and he did exactly as the young bishop asked. Faithfully."

"Wow!" I exclaimed, authentically impressed, "And she was cured of the cancer?"

"Zannoni tells me that hers is one of the miracles being examined for Padre Pio's canonization cause. She was literally on the operating table; the doctors hoped to remove part of the tumor obstructing her internal organs. As I say, moments before they cut her open, the same doctors who had found the tumors could find no trace of them any longer. Not one blessed trace!"

"Her name," Gagnon smiled, "is Doctor Poltawska; Doctor Wanda Poltawska."

"You know her?" Marini asked with surprise.

"I know of her —from Zannoni, of course. He tells me that she's in Rome. Zannoni called and asked me if I wanted to speak with Doctor Poltawska; that perhaps she would speak to the pope about seeing me sooner rather than later. I thanked him for his offer of help. But I've decided to tackle this on my own." Then Gagnon asked me, "Are you free tomorrow morning?"

"I'll make myself free," I answered.

"Good. If you could drive me to the Vatican, please, around ten o'clock. I don't have an appointment, but I've never needed one to perform a corporal work of mercy."

"Excellency?" I asked what he meant.

"I think I'll pay Cardinal Villot a visit, in person. I'll walk into his office unannounced, and demand an official and private audience with the pope. At the same time, I'll be visiting the sick."

"Let's hope you don't leave him sicker than you found him," Marini said.

The following morning, Monday, January 15, 1979, was the third time in eight months that I was driving Archbishop Édouard Joseph Gagnon to the Cortile San Damaso, and all three times for the same reason: that the Apostolic Visitor to the Roman Curia, commissioned by Paul VI to conduct the most comprehensive investigation into the central offices of the Catholic Church since their establishment in 1588, might present the results of his three-year study to the Pope.

Archbishop Eduard Gagnon looked very grave as I drove him to his non-appointment with the dying Secretary of State. I observed, "When Villot looks up and sees you standing there, in the doorway to his office, the shock might kill the poor fellow right then and there."

"You underestimate our French cardinal, my good Don Carlo," Gagnon grinned, "A Canadian archbishop at his door might get his attention briefly - and that archbishop will have to talk fast if he wants his short message delivered in full. The main thing I want to do this morning is register a formal complaint against the Secretariat of State. I will charge that the report delivered to Pope John Paul the First has not been seen by Pope John Paul the Second; that the Secretariat has withheld it from the new pope intentionally, to prevent him from seeing for himself, firsthand, the appalling state of the Roman Curia today."

"May I ask a question?"

"Certainly."

"Where is Cardinal Benelli in all of this? Why isn't he rattling a few cages? Wojtyla was his man. What's more, Wojtyla has even stated that he himself voted all the way for Benelli! So where is Benelli? Why hasn't he stepped up to the plate and helped you? Has he even been back in Rome since the election?"

"Once, that I know of," Gagnon responded lugubriously. "We met. We talked. We agreed: this pope is off to a very bad start," he stated and shook his head, "Reappointing every Curial department head to his same position —a major mistake. He told me to phone Cardinal Villot and to insist on an audience with the Holy Father. 'Alone,' he cautioned. I have phoned his office several times. Left messages. Nothing."

"No, no, no," he said, shaking his head. "It's an age-old, ironclad rule: New pope, new Curia; new pontificate, new administration. As President of the Committee for the Family, I wrote out my resignation and sent it to the pope the day after his election. He should have replaced me with someone of his own liking, someone he knew personally and trusted completely. Or, if he actually wanted me, for me, he should have reconfirmed me - but me, as an individual, not an across the board 'everybody, stay where you are' confirmation! It's not only absurd and not done, it's dangerous. And in the cases of Villot and Baggio, it is extremely detrimental to keep them right where they were... a terrible misstep... grave mistake. It's as if he considers the Church's central government to be of tertiary importance."

"Then, what do you consider his primary and secondary concerns to be?"

Édouard Gagnon remained silent for a while. "Poland's liberation from Communism is his primary concern... a noble cause, to be sure, but not the reason he was elected Pastor of the Church universal," he frowned.

"And in second place?"

"Traveling," he answered flatly. "He leaves for Mexico, the Dominican Republic and the Bahamas in two weeks. And I hear that Villot and Casaroli are already doing the preliminaries for a trip to Poland. Again, very noble causes — bringing the Lord and His Gospel to the poor but..."

"But?"

"Ou chat na rat regne," he responded in French.

"Yes," I agreed, "but while the cat's away, the rats have their superiors to answer to, n'est pas?"

"You're French is good," he nodded and smiled. "And your Latin, Don Carlo?"

"Go ahead," I laughed, "Hit me with all you've got!"

"Quis custodiet ipsos custodes?" the former Latin professor put forth the question from Juvenal.

"Who guards..." I started off pretty well, I thought, "themselves... guards well!?" I answered and asked at the same time. I knew I had blown it.

"You proposed that the rats will obey their superiors."

"Yes?"

"And I ask you: 'Quis custodiet ipsos custodes?' — 'Who will guard' — future tense," he corrected me, 'the guards themselves?' You would leave the guards, Villot, Casaroli, and Baggio, to guard themselves? Good gracious, man! I can willingly overlook rusty Latin, but, Don Carlino, what happened to your reasoning!?"

I laughed and looked over to see my Canadian friend fighting off the temptation to smile.

We arrived at the Vatican and when we reached Cortile San Damaso, I left Archbishop Gagnon off and watched him walk toward the elevator to the Secretariat. I waited for what I thought would be his swift return.

And I was right. In less than twenty minutes he was back in the car.

"Was he surprised to see you?" I ask.

"I gave my name to the porter — of course, he remembered me from my interview with him during the investigation— and then I walked past him and straight down to Villot's office. I was determined not to give him the chance to tell the porter that he wasn't there, or that he was busy. ... I take no delight in saying this, but when he saw me standing in his doorway —I believe he was inhaling at the time— the poor man went into a coughing jag that took a full minute for him to get under control.

"The Holy Father will see me as soon as he returns from Mexico," he added, very pleased with the day, indeed.

"That's sensational news. Sensational!"

For a moment neither of us spoke.

"You smoke, don't you?"

"Mostly when I write, but, yes, I do," I answered.

"What brand?"

"Parliaments," I answered.

"Promise me one thing, Don Carlo," he said almost pleadingly.

"You know, Excellency, that if I can, I will."

"Don't worry," he rolled his eyes, "I won't ask you to

quit. But do promise me this: you'll never take up smoking Gauloise!"

"You have my word on that!" I promised, and grinned.

THE THIRD DELIVERY ATTEMPT

February 6, 1979[1]

"Your Fiat might legally and technically require a driver, Excellency," I said as I turned the ignition key, "but I'll bet, if you asked it politely, it could find its own way from here to the Holy Office gates, around the basilica, and right up to the elevator landing in Cortile San Damaso."

"It's not a day for taking chances," he joshed back, "I'd still rather you drive," he said with a smile, "It's slightly safer and if anyone can make up for lost time, it's Don Carlo."

This was the third time that Archbishop Édouard Joseph Gagnon was meeting with a pope to present and discuss the results of his investigation of the Roman Curia. I always gave us ample traveling time, but the phone call threw us off. Sister Jean de la Croix stopped us as we were leaving the house to tell Archbishop Gagnon that the Archbishop of Florence, Cardinal Benelli, was on the phone and asked to speak with him. Naturally, Gagnon took what turned out to be a ten-minute call.

"I'll get you there on time," I told him, "But please, no complaints about the short-cuts."

"I had to take his call. It was very important."

"No doubt, it was, Excellency," I answered, "I just don't

1 Author's Note: In an interview with *Inside the Vatican* in November, 2020, I mistakenly said that the meeting between Pope St. John Paul II and Archbishop Gagnon took place in October, 1978.

want you late for a private papal audience that you've been waiting for since the sixteenth of October, 1978!"

"Almost four months," he sighed, "Four months for the busy scoundrels desperate to cover their tracks. It seems our Nuncio to Iran has an urgent need 'to explain himself' to the new pontiff; he cannot wait until diplomatic protocol calls him to Rome. It has to be now."

"Bugnini?"

"The same. And the same advocating for him."

"Cardinal Villot," I stated rather than asked.

"Cardinals Villot and Baggio," he corrected, "They want him back in Rome, if you can imagine such a thing. They want the pope to receive him and say: 'All is forgiven; we've killed the fatted calf; come home, dear son.'"

"But he's a Freemason," I protested strongly, "Why they sent him to Iran instead of straight to hell makes no sense to me. It never has, and it never will."

"I explained all that to you, already," said the archbishop, "It was done to avoid further scandal. That, at least, was the answer I received when I ask the very same question you just asked — the very same question Cardinal Staffa asked… and Cardinal Oddi asked… and Benelli asked."

Upon arrival, it was the same routine. We were waved through the narrow archways and saluted by the Swiss Guards when entering San Damaso Courtyard. I opened the passenger door and helped Gagnon out. It was February and there was a cold wind in the air. Upon his shoulders, over his purple-piped cassock, sash and zucchetto, I put his black woolen overcoat. I did not hand him his black leather book bag, but rather carried it for him as I accompanied him to the elevator. Unlike my previous attempts to help him with these weighty and explosive documents, this time he accepted the favor without protest.

In cassock and collar, and knowing my way around

perfectly well, with the guard's permission I left the car parked to one side of the courtyard and proceeded to the Instituto per le Opere di Religione, a.k.a., the Vatican Bank, to withdraw some needed funds from my account.

The Catholic world may have changed popes three times since last I saw the Bank President, Archbishop Paul Marcinkus, but you certainly wouldn't know it by the looks of him and those around him. I walked past his open office door and saw him, seated behind his desk, in the middle of a phone conversation. Nothing had really changed. Nothing, it seemed, ever would, or ever could. Everything was as everything always was. It was as Mario Marini always said: "Popes come and go; the Roman Curia remains."

Would what Archbishop Gagnon was presenting at this very moment to the new pope change anything? I hoped so. I really hoped so. After I finished my business in the bank, not knowing how long Archbishop Gagnon would be with the Holy Father, I returned to the car to be ready and waiting for him the moment he appeared.

Having finished Lauds and Lectio Divina, I was almost through a third rosary when the shrill sound of the guard's metal whistle got my attention. I got out of the car and hurried toward Gagnon to take his much lighter bag.

Very out of character for him, he said nothing until we were in the car.

"Please, Don Carlo, would you be so kind as to take me right home — the sooner we get there, the better."

And then there was total silence — a silence I respected and guarded almost as a sacred duty. Did I understand it? I clearly interpreted his tone, his expression, and his silence symptomatic of a migraine headache. I deduced that the audience between the Apostolic Visitor and the new pope had not gone as he had hoped. Without moving my head, I caught glimpses of my friend's pained expression and I could see that the audience had gone very poorly — no, the audience had been a disaster.

The archbishop broke his silence as we neared the residence.

"Could I impose on you one last time, Don Carlo?"

"No such thing exists when it comes to helping you, Excellency. Tell me."

"I want you to drive me to the airport tomorrow."

"You're taking a trip?"

"I'm leaving Rome — leaving the Vatican. Let them wallow in their corruption if that be their will. As for me, I will not be a part of it one day longer."

"But, Excellency," I began.

"Save it, Don Carlo. My mind is made up. Are you free tomorrow?"

"You can count on me," I said as a sadness began to invade me.

We arrived home. Gagnon went directly to his room, without lunch, to lie down.

I followed his example.

Archbishop Paul Marcinkus

A MORE CIVILIZED JUNGLE

February 8, 1979

It was only nine-thirty that Thursday morning, and although Archbishop Gagnon's flight for New York wasn't scheduled to depart until one-thirty in the afternoon, he was anxious to get going. I thought I understood: the good man had made up his mind, and now all he wanted was the greatest distance between himself and anything even remotely reminiscent of the Vatican and its Roman Curia. Being forced into such close proximity these past years with the rotting underbelly of the beast, *and* all to no avail, was too much even for the strongest man of faith to endure. This kind of devil - as his Colombian friends were fond of saying —had no mother.

"OK, then," he said as he gave the final once-over to his room, "That, as they say, is that!" With a quick and satisfied nod of the head, he bent to pick up his only suitcase, but I fought him for it and won.

"You've got all your travel documents and tickets in your briefcase, right?" I asked.

"All present and accounted for, sir," he said in his best American accent.

"You know, Excellency, it's too soon to be leaving for the airport right now. I don't want you sitting alone for three hours. Why don't we go to the café around the corner for coffee and a chat?"

He pursed his lips together, as he always did when he was about to propose something.

"I have another favor to ask of you, Don Carlo. Just imagine: when you drop me off at the airport, you'll finally be free of this troublesome old man."

"Don't say that, Excellency, even in jest. Besides, since when do sixty-one years 'an old man make'? What is it you need done?"

"Very well, then. Let me take full advantage of your noble generosity," he said and again pursed his lips, "...I wanted to leave a littler earlier today because I need to pay one final visit — a *visita finale* — to the Vatican Secretariat."

"Seems like only yesterday," I joked.

"No," he smiled, "It was twice as long as that; it was the day before yesterday," he laughed, "We have time for that, no?"

"We have time for that, yes," I confirmed.

"There's another small errand I would like you to run for me - but I can explain that in the car, on the way to Villot."

"You're going to see Cardinal Villot?"

"Well, yes, sort of," he said and looked around the room one last time. "Plenty of good talks within these four walls, no?"

"To be sure," I agreed.

"I left you what remains of the *aguardiente*. There should be enough for two drinks to my safe return to Colombia. Maybe you and Mario would drink to that before you retire tonight?"

"We're going to miss you a lot, Excellency," I said and felt a tightening in my throat that didn't permit me to speak another word.

A knock on the open door revealed a small committee of well-wishers headed by our very own Archbishop Hilarion Capucci, fully attired right down to the brass-knobbed walking-stick. Behind him stood the house superior, Soeur

Jean de la Croix, the greatest cook in the entire Near East, Soeur Olga, and the kindly nun who tended to the priests' rooms, Soeur Marina. Archbishop Capucci delivered a short discourse in French and the sisters, one by one, said their tearful goodbyes to one of the saintliest, kindest, cheerful, and least demanding clerics they had ever known.

As we walked down the corridor to the elevator, I pretended not to notice the tears in Archbishop Gagnon's eyes.

And so we began our last drive to the *Cortile San Damaso.*

As we passed the Swiss Guards at the Holy Office gates of Vatican City, and headed to the final climb around the basilica, from the vest pocket of his black coat Édouard Joseph Gagnon took out a sealed envelope and clutched it in his hands.

As soon as I had pulled right up to the steps to the elevator landing, as I was about to get out and open the archbishop's door for him, Gagnon took my right forearm with his left hand to stop me and with his right hand handed me the mysterious white envelope.

"I knew there was something I'd forgotten to ask you," he said with a mischievous smile, "Would you be so kind as to take this up to the Secretariat? Tell the porter at the desk that Archbishop Gagnon asks that it be delivered immediately to His Eminence, Cardinal Villot, and to His Eminence alone."

"But Excellency," I began to protest, "Look at me;" I said, "in khakis and a sweatshirt! I can't just waltz into the Secretariat looking like this! Why didn't you say something while we were at home? I could have…"

"Because you'd have put on a cassock and a fresh starched collar. No," he said emphatically, "I'm asking you to deliver this just as you are. Nothing special. It's Jean Villot you might run into; not the King of Denmark, Charlie," he instructed and, one of the rarest times since he'd ordained me, called me by my first name; my nickname.

"But what am I supposed to say? What if Villot *is* there and asks me something? What if he asks me where you are?"

'You tell him, *please,*" he politely added and with the slightest bow of the head, "that I am in my car in the *Cortile San Damaso*, and am on my way to Leonardo Da Vinci Airport."

"But..."

"I want nothing more to do with the Secretariat of State or with its Prefect. I don't want to go up there, nor do I want anyone from on high lowering himself by coming to me. Period. Can you do this for me, Charlie? Do you think you can handle it?"

"You're sure this is what you want?"

"Quite sure, thank you."

I shook my head and had to take a deep breath. Then I started to put the car in reverse to park it where I always did, next to the courtyard's side wall.

"No need for that," Gagnon said with a dismissive wave of his hand, "I'll wait for you right here. It shouldn't take but five minutes. Please, just see that Villot gets my letter of resignation and let's get out of here."

Before I knew it, I was inside the wood-paneled elevator, standing between two well-dressed *Monsignori*, with my head down, hoping that no one from the Information Office or anyone else I knew saw me. I felt I was actually in a dream I used to have occasionally, where I arrived at school only to realize, before God and the world, that I'd forgotten to put on my pants that morning!

I walked the long loggia with quickened pace and lowered gaze, as if I were a worker examining the marble floors for cracks. When I arrived to the reception area, I stood before the seated, middle-aged porter, the same man that Mario Marini never trusted. It was easy to see why. His *"antipatico"* was glaringly evident. I remembered him well enough, and, at this uncomfortable moment, hoped he did not remember me.

"Buongiorno, Signore," I began.

"And to you, sir," he answered.

"I have a letter from His Excellency, Archbishop Édouard Gagnon to the Secretary of State, His Eminence, Cardinal Jean Villot. The archbishop instructs me to deliver it to His Eminence and requests that he open and read it immediately." I then repeated with added *gravitas*: "The contents are meant for the eyes of His Eminence alone."

The porter took the envelope.

"Wait here," he said, "Take a seat," he said and pointed to several chairs lined against the wall in the less than spacious room.

"I prefer to stand, thank you."

This was the first time in almost a year that I had returned to the Secretariat. It was a strange, unsure feeling to be standing there now. Benelli was no longer the powerhouse "in charge of the world" —and, from what the new pontiff led Gagnon to believe, he would not be returning again, even after the imminent demise of Villot. Zannoni was no longer here, since Villot had him transferred to the Congregation for the Clergy. Of course, since Villot had dismissed the "Benelli spy," Mario Marini was absent as well.

I was uncomfortable at standing there not properly attired; more, I was extremely ill at ease being there at all. I decided that I had completed what I was sent to do and had waited long enough.

I turned and walked out through the ancient doorway to the wide loggia whose tall, solid wall of windows bathed the entire Apostolic Palace in brilliant sunlight. On my way down the corridor, I looked up at the Renaissance ceiling and fondly remembered Mario Marini, years ago, explaining each panel of the road to salvation, one way, and the road to perdition, the other.

"Where is he?" I heard a loud, unhappy voice.

"He was here a moment ago, Your Eminence," the unfriendly porter answered.

"You there!" the porter's voice rang out more clearly.

As I was the only person in the loggia at the moment, I stopped, turned, and saw the porter standing ten feet away; next to him, haggard-looking and scowling, stood His Eminence, Cardinal Jean Villot.

"Did you mean me, *Signore?*" I asked in the meekest voice I could muster.

"His Eminence wants a word with you."

I walked back to where he stood as the porter slid back to his post.

"Where is he?" snapped Villot.

"Archbishop Gagnon?" I asked like a lost simpleton.

"Of course, Gagnon. Where is he?" he demanded.

"In his car. In the cortile."

"Tell him to come to my office at once."

I found both the man's tone and attitude offensive, and I could feel my own temperature rising. I struggled to keep my head because I wanted to represent Archbishop Édouard Gagnon the way he deserved to be represented.

"With all due respect, Your Eminence, His Excellency declines your invitation."

"Declines my invitation!? I made no — no invitation!" he sputtered, "Tell him he's to report to my office at once. Now!" he demanded and immediately went into a fit of deep coughing — so much so that the porter returned with a glass of water and a handkerchief. It was no act; this was a very sick man.

When he regained control of himself, I assured him

that the archbishop would not come up; that he refused to speak with him or anyone else from his department.

"And just who are you?" he asked and coughed several more times. "I, I know you. From where do I know you?" he asked and then put the handkerchief to his mouth.

"I can't imagine, Your Eminence," I answered as politely as I could, "I don't recall ever having made your acquaintance."

"Where is he going?" Villot managed to get out.

"I'm not sure," I shrugged my shoulders, "He mentioned something about returning to Colombia — to the 'much more civilized jungles' of Colombia, he called them. And you know, of course, how devoted he is to the Sacred Heart of Jesus. Maybe those facts will narrow down your search efforts."

Cardinal Villot's eyes widened and again he began coughing, much more violently than before. "Can I get you something, Eminence?" I asked obligingly. "Shall I call a priest?" I meant one of the dozens of clerics who staffed his Secretariat, but his expression suggested I meant a priest to give him the last rites. The porter returned and took him by the arm, but Villot shooed him away as he continued coughing into the white cloth over his nose and mouth.

Taking this as a most opportune moment to leave, I bowed and bid him: "*Addio e buona continuazione [Goodbye and may everything go along well for you]*," then turned, and made my way to the waiting elevator.

Naturally, as soon as I got back behind the wheel of Gagnon's Fiat *Mirafiori* and pulled out of the *Cortile San Damaso*, I commenced a detailed report of my adventure upstairs and Cardinal Jean Villot's reaction to the archbishop's letter. I made it a lively narrative, hoping to lift his spirits; and, as hard as he tried not to smile, more than once he failed. Nor could he hold back a chuckle over my suggestion that I call a priest for the cardinal. However, as much as both of us had reason to dislike the Frenchman —Gagnon far more than me - neither he nor I took the least bit of pleasure in his worsening health. In fact, when Archbishop Gagnon said most earnestly that he would offer his next Mass for the cardinal's spiritual and physical wellbeing, I agreed to do the same.

From the *Via Aurelia* we got onto the highway and were within twenty minutes of our destination.

"May I ask you a question?" I asked my passenger.

"Of course," he answered, "What is it?"

"Last night, at the *trattoria*, you said there was something else you told the Holy Father in your audience with him. Not about the bank. Not about Baggio. There was a third major topic you brought up with him."

"How attentive you are to detail, Don Carlo," he smiled and paused before continuing to speak, "Yes. It was something that was not part of my investigation… In fact, I was only informed of it the night before my audience with the Holy Father."

Though he did not say it, I assumed it was something important communicated to him in one of the several last-minute calls to and from Cardinal Giovanni Benelli.

"I informed His Holiness of a foiled plot to assassinate him," he said in very matter of fact fashion, "and that his life was in constant danger from enemies from behind the iron curtain."

"Holy Mother!" I exclaimed.

"He doubted the veracity of the claim. He asked me, in all seriousness: 'Who in the world would want to kill the Pope of Rome?' He completely dismissed it. Can you imagine?" Gagnon was still flabbergasted at the man's naïveté, "Without giving too much thought to the matter, I could come up with a sizeable list of candidates, many inside the Vatican itself, who would like to see him eliminated already! God save the Church…"

A curious melancholy invaded our final moments together. We hardly spoke until we reached the airport's main terminal.

"...And the car, Excellency?" I asked.

"Oh my, yes, the car!" he exclaimed, "Pierpaolo from the office will be in touch with you. He'll come for it and take it to the Vatican garage on the *Via dei Corridori*. Not Trastevere; *Via dei Corridori*. You might remind him of that. I'm so glad you thought of it! God help me, I'm getting so forgetful."

"Only because you have a ton and a half of awful things you had to learn — all of them crying to be forgotten and never called to mind again!" I said gravely.

I got out of the car, popped the truck and took out his one, heavy suitcase. I called a baggage-man with an empty luggage trolley and paid him to accompany the archbishop to his check-in desk.

"There are a lot of good people here who will miss you tremendously. I will miss you especially, Excellency. I admire your faith... your courage... your honesty and your conviction...

"Will I ever see you again?" I asked, almost moved to tears at the thought of losing this great man of God, this wonderful defender of the faith.

"If God wills it, Charlie; if God wills it."

"Your blessing, please," I asked, and knelt to receive it.

As I watched him leaving, before he might forever be lost from my sight, from somewhere just below my heart came the urge to shout out: *"Et voilà, Monseigneur...!"*

The man in the floppy black hat and trench coat stopped and turned back. He removed his hat and, waving it, smiled and shouted back to me: *"...pourquoi votre fille est muette!!"*

Father Charles Theodore Murr

EPILOGUE

As I bring my chronicle to a close, I would like to inform the reader briefly of the subsequent history of each of the characters.

Cardinal Jean-Marie VILLOT, Secretary of the Vatican State, friend to Sebastiano Baggio, enemy to Giovanni Benelli, died (bronchial pneumonia; lung cancer) on March 9, 1979, one month after being handed Édouard Gagnon's letter of resignation.

Monsignor Mario MARINI was found not guilty of the 1978 charges leveled against him by then-Secretary of State Cardinal Jean Villot. Pope John Paul II assigned Marini to the Congregation for the Clergy, where he worked with his friend and Secretary of that Congregation, Monsignor Guglielmo Zannoni. Pope Benedict XVI named him Secretary of the Sacred Congregation for Divine Worship (ironically, the position held at one time by Annibale Bugnini.) Pope Benedict also named him Secretary of the *Ecclesia Dei Commission*, which was created to assist those affiliated with Archbishop Marcel Lefevre to separate themselves from the influence of the Society of St. Pius X in order to be officially recognized by the Holy See. This possibly was aimed at weakening the position of the SSPX, but, paradoxically, by permitting the sacred patrimony of the pre-conciliar liturgy to be more accessible to the faithful, both the SSPX and the new groups of traditional faithful flourished. In an effort to move him from Rome, on two occasions Cardinal Baggio offered him prestigious dioceses in northern Italy. Monsignor Marini declined. He died of liver cancer, May 24, 2009.

Archbishop Édouard Joseph GAGNON resigned as President of the Pontifical Commission for the Family, and left the Vatican to work among the poor in Colombia, offering Mass, administering the Sacraments, and directing spiritual retreats.

In early 1981, the Italian Secret Police informed Pope John Paul II that in a raid on the Grand Masonic Lodge [*Propaganda Due* (P2)], they uncovered a Masonic plot to bankrupt the Vatican. In May of that same year, a would-be assassin's bullets left the pontiff fighting for his life in the Gemelli Hospital. When John Paul II regained consciousness and the power of speech, it was said that the first two words out of his mouth were: "F-i-n-d G-a-g-n-o-n…"

After an extensive search, Secretary of State Agostino Casaroli located the Canadian prelate exactly where he always said he would be, but the last place Vatican bureaucracy thought to look for him: with the poor, deep within the Colombian interior.

The archbishop flew back to Rome and met privately with the pope. As he told me many times: "His Holiness seemed much more interested in the results of my investigation than he had been when last we spoke of the same matters," [i.e., in 1979, two years prior to the assassination attempt and the bank implosion].

Pope John Paul II wanted Archbishop Gagnon to return to Rome, but (given all that he had come to know from his investigation), the French-Canadian presented two conditions for his return: the removal of Cardinal Baggio from the Congregation for Bishops and of Bishop Paul Marcinkus from the Vatican Bank. I was privileged to be seated in Saint Peter's Square, right behind "my Canadian Father," when, in the consistory of 1985, Pope John Paul

II placed a cardinal's red hat upon the head of Édouard Joseph Gagnon.

We spoke for the last time on August 22, 2007. I attended his Requiem in Notre Dame and burial at *Le Grand Seminaire de Montreal*.

Cardinal Giovanni BENELLI was asked by Pope John Paul II to serve as Vatican Secretary of State in 1982. Cardinal Benelli willingly acceded to the pontiff's request and returned to Florence to ready things for his departure from the Archdiocese and his return to the Vatican Secretariat. Ten days after his private audience with the Holy Father – Gagnon himself told me – Giovanni Benelli suffered a massive heart attack. He died in his residence at sixty-one years of age.

Cardinal Sebastiano BAGGIO was prematurely relieved of his position as Prefect of the Sacred Congregation for Bishops in 1984, and was replaced by Cardinal Giovanni Benelli's African friend and protégé, Cardinal Bernard Gantin. Baggio was named President of the Pontifical Commission for Vatican City State, an appointment reported in the press as a clear demotion. He died in 1993.

Archbishop Annibale BUGNINI remained in exile in Iran for the remainder of his life. He did return to Rome for medical reasons and died there on July 3, 1982.

Archbishop Hilarion CAPUCCI and I met for breakfast whenever I returned to Rome. The last time I saw him was in 2016. My most memorable visit was in April, 1980. He asked me at breakfast to pray for a very special intention. That evening on the news there was film of him blessing the flag-draped caskets of the eight Marines killed in a failed attempt to rescue 53 hostages in Tehran. He later explained that President Carter, in a desperate effort to communicate with the Ayatollah Khomeini, had telephoned Pope John Paul. The Holy Father asked Archbishop Capucci to act.

With his blessing and the approval of the Syrian Ambassador to the United Nations, I was allowed to write a book (*The Syrian*) about a few very intense days in 1983 when he and I joined forces to ransom a kidnap victim in Beirut. Archbishop Hilarion Capucci died in 2018 at his home in EUR; he was 94 years old.

Father Charles Theodore MURR is the last man standing of the characters in this book. He misses each of those intriguingly remarkable people and those extraordinary times. With great fondness he remembers "the Roman years," and with singular affection and longing, "the Year of the Three Popes."

Made in the USA
Las Vegas, NV
06 November 2024

11235202R00129